LEGENDS OF A

YORUBA, DOGON, ZULU & AKAN MYTHOLOGY

4 BOOKS IN 1

BOOK 1
YORUBA MYTHOLOGY: ORISHAS AND ORIGINS: THE SACRED TALES OF YORUBA MYTHOLOGY

BOOK 2
DOGON MYTHOLOGY: STARS AND SPIRITS: THE MYSTICAL WORLD OF DOGON MYTHOLOGY

BOOK 3
ZULU MYTHOLOGY: THUNDERS OF THE SKY: THE MYTHS AND LEGENDS OF ZULU GODS

BOOK 4
AKAN MYTHOLOGY: ANANSI'S WEB: STORIES AND DEITIES OF AKAN MYTHOLOGY

SAMUEL SHEPHERD

Copyright © 2024 by Samuel Shepherd
All rights reserved. No part of this book may be reproduced or transmitted in any form or by any means, electronic or mechanical, including photocopying, recording, or by any information storage and retrieval system, without permission in writing from the publisher.

Published by Samuel Shepherd
Library of Congress Cataloging-in-Publication Data
ISBN 978-1-83938-890-3
Cover design by Rizzo

Disclaimer

The contents of this book are based on extensive research and the best available historical sources. However, the author and publisher make no claims, promises, or guarantees about the accuracy, completeness, or adequacy of the information contained herein. The information in this book is provided on an "as is" basis, and the author and publisher disclaim any and all liability for any errors, omissions, or inaccuracies in the information or for any actions taken in reliance on such information. The opinions and views expressed in this book are those of the author and do not necessarily reflect the official policy or position of any organization or individual mentioned in this book. Any reference to specific people, places, or events is intended only to provide historical context and is not intended to defame or malign any group, individual, or entity. The information in this book is intended for educational and entertainment purposes only. It is not intended to be a substitute for professional advice or judgment. Readers are encouraged to conduct their own research and to seek professional advice where appropriate. Every effort has been made to obtain necessary permissions and acknowledgments for all images and other copyrighted material used in this book. Any errors or omissions in this regard are unintentional, and the author and publisher will correct them in future editions.

BOOK 1 - YORUBA MYTHOLOGY: ORISHAS AND ORIGINS: THE SACRED TALES OF YORUBA MYTHOLOGY

Introduction 5
Chapter 1: The Beginning of All Things 9
Chapter 2: Descent of the Orishas 13
Chapter 3: Obatala's Vision 17
Chapter 4: Shango, Thunder and Fire 21
Chapter 5: Oshun: Goddess of Love and Rivers 25
Chapter 6: Esu: The Trickster's Path 29
Chapter 7: Oya: Queen of Winds and Change 33
Chapter 8: Ogun: The Forge of War and Creation 38
Chapter 9: Healing and Divination 42
Chapter 10: The Eternal Legacy of the Orishas 47

BOOK 2 - DOGON MYTHOLOGY: STARS AND SPIRITS: THE MYSTICAL WORLD OF DOGON MYTHOLOGY

Chapter 1: In the Beginning of Time 53
Chapter 2: Amma, the Supreme Creator 58
Chapter 3: The Birth of the Nommo 63
Chapter 4: Sirius and the Cosmic Connection 68
Chapter 5: The Sacred Role of Twins 72
Chapter 6: The Symbols of Earth and Sky 76
Chapter 7: Spirits of the Ancestors 80
Chapter 8: Rituals of Fertility and Harvest 85
Chapter 9: Masks, Dances, and Divine Communication 90
Chapter 10: The Dogon Mysteries and Modern Fascination 95

BOOK 3 - ZULU MYTHOLOGY: THUNDERS OF THE SKY: THE MYTHS AND LEGENDS OF ZULU GODS

Chapter 1: In the Beginning of Time 101
Chapter 2: Amma, the Supreme Creator 104
Chapter 3: The Birth of the Nommo 109
Chapter 4: Sirius and the Cosmic Connection 114
Chapter 5: The Sacred Role of Twins 119
Chapter 6: The Symbols of Earth and Sky 124
Chapter 7: Spirits of the Ancestors 129
Chapter 8: Rituals of Fertility and Harvest 134
Chapter 9: Masks, Dances, and Divine Communication 139
Chapter 10: The Dogon Mysteries and Modern Fascination 144

BOOK 4 - AKAN MYTHOLOGY: ANANSI'S WEB: STORIES AND DEITIES OF AKAN MYTHOLOGY

Chapter 1: Nyame, the Supreme Sky God 150
Chapter 2: The Creation of the World 155
Chapter 3: Asase Yaa: Mother Earth and Fertility 160
Chapter 4: Anansi the Spider: Trickster and Storyteller 165
Chapter 5: Bia and Tano: Guardians of Nature 170
Chapter 6: Spirits of the Forest and River 175
Chapter 7: The Wisdom of Ancestral Spirits 180
Chapter 8: Myths of Justice and Morality 185
Chapter 9: Folktales of Wisdom and Cunning 190
Chapter 10: Anansi's Legacy in Akan Culture and Beyond 195
Conclusion 200

Introduction

Legends of Africa: Yoruba, Dogon, Zulu & Akan Mythology is a journey into the heart of Africa's ancient wisdom and rich spiritual heritage. This collection introduces readers to four of the continent's most enduring and complex mythological traditions: the sacred tales of Yoruba deities and the Orishas; the celestial mysteries of the Dogon and their connection to the stars; the powerful, sky-reaching myths of the Zulu; and the cunning, wise stories of Anansi and the Akan. Each mythology offers a glimpse into the deep reverence these cultures hold for nature, the universe, and the unseen forces that guide human life.

In Africa, mythology is more than storytelling; it is a living, breathing force that weaves together community values, spiritual beliefs, and personal identity. African myths are passed down through oral tradition, forming the foundation of each culture's understanding of the world, the cosmos, and humanity's place within it. These myths, both intimate and grand, reveal how the Yoruba, Dogon, Zulu, and Akan peoples have defined concepts of creation, morality, community, and the divine. Far from being relics of the past, these stories continue to shape the spiritual and moral framework of these societies, connecting the past with the present and offering lessons that remain relevant today.

In *Book 1*, *Yoruba Mythology: Orishas and Origins*, we explore the vibrant pantheon of the Yoruba, where gods and goddesses known as Orishas influence every part of life. Each Orisha embodies unique qualities and powers, and their stories reveal the Yoruba's profound respect for balance, nature, and harmony. Through the lives of Orunmila, Shango, Oshun, and other Orishas, we glimpse a world where deities walk among people, teach lessons, and intervene in human affairs.

Book 2, *Dogon Mythology: Stars and Spirits*, takes us into the mystical world of the Dogon people, who hold an astonishing understanding of the cosmos, particularly the Sirius star system. Through tales of the Nommo, spiritual amphibious beings who descended from the heavens, we uncover the Dogon's complex view of creation, ancestral reverence, and the unity between Earth and sky. This book celebrates the Dogon's unique perspective on life and the universe, showing us a tradition deeply rooted in mystery, knowledge, and cosmic interconnectedness.

In *Book 3*, *Zulu Mythology: Thunders of the Sky*, we encounter the powerful sky gods and legendary figures of the Zulu people. The stories here are filled with fierce warriors, wise ancestors, and the forces of nature, revealing a tradition that reveres courage, respect, and loyalty. These tales reflect the Zulu's connection to the land, the skies, and the strength that binds their communities. Through thunderous gods and heroic legends, the Zulu myths teach us about resilience and the importance of unity.

Finally, *Book 4*, *Akan Mythology: Anansi's Web*, explores the vibrant tales of Anansi the Spider, the ultimate trickster and storyteller. Anansi's cleverness and wit capture the essence of Akan wisdom and resilience, using humor and cunning to navigate life's challenges. His stories, though lighthearted, convey deep lessons about humility, cooperation, and the power of storytelling itself. Anansi's legacy continues to inspire across Africa and the diaspora, reminding us of the enduring wisdom held within Akan culture.

Legends of Africa invites readers to delve into these sacred traditions, celebrating the diversity and depth of African mythology. Through the Yoruba, Dogon, Zulu, and Akan perspectives, we encounter universal themes of love, bravery, faith, and the search for truth, woven into tales that continue to inspire, teach, and captivate. This book is a tribute to the timeless power of myth and the legacy of African spirituality, offering readers a chance to explore the ancestral wisdom that remains a guiding light in African culture and beyond.

BOOK 1
YORUBA MYTHOLOGY
ORISHAS AND ORIGINS: THE SACRED TALES OF
YORUBA MYTHOLOGY
SAMUEL SHEPHERD

Chapter 1: The Beginning of All Things

In Yoruba mythology, the story of creation is a deeply significant narrative, reflecting both the Yoruba worldview and their understanding of the cosmos. At the heart of this myth lies Olodumare, the supreme being and source of all creation. Olodumare is considered both omnipotent and omniscient, embodying the beginning and the end, yet he remains distant, allowing the Orishas, a pantheon of divine beings, to serve as intermediaries and agents of his will in the world. Olodumare is believed to have created the heavens, the earth, and the realm of humanity, laying the foundation for a world that is both orderly and interwoven with the divine.

The Yoruba creation myth tells that Olodumare, in his vast wisdom, decided to bring the world into existence, beginning with the sky and earth, which were initially in a formless state. However, to bring balance and life to the earth, Olodumare appointed Obatala, one of the most revered Orishas, as the creator of humankind and the shaper of the physical world. Obatala was tasked with descending from the heavens to form the land and mold the first human beings. He took with him a golden chain to climb down from the heavens, a bag of sand, and a hen. These items were sacred and essential to the creation process, each carrying symbolic significance in Yoruba cosmology.

Obatala began his descent, climbing down the golden chain until he reached a suitable place to start creating land. At a particular spot where the sky and earth met, Obatala released the bag of sand and let it spill onto the formless earth. He then placed the hen on top of the sand, and as the hen scratched and spread the sand across the surface, it created mountains, valleys, and plains, forming the landscape of the world. This act symbolized the development of the natural world, a place where life could eventually thrive and evolve. The act of spreading sand with a hen represents the idea of creation from chaos, as something as simple as scattered sand could be molded into organized landforms by the work of an intentional creator.

Obatala, however, was not the only Orisha involved in the creation of the world. Ogun, the god of iron and war, played a significant role in ensuring that the physical world would be protected and maintained. Known for his strength and resilience, Ogun provided Obatala with tools crafted from iron, essential for shaping the land and forming its boundaries. Ogun's iron tools symbolized the structure and discipline needed to keep chaos at bay, a theme that permeates Yoruba beliefs. These tools allowed Obatala to mold the earth effectively, marking Ogun as a guardian of both creation and order.

As Obatala began shaping the first humans, he made a decision to sculpt each human from the clay of the earth. This clay was sacred, a gift from Olodumare, and served as the physical vessel for the spiritual essence of human life. However, during the creation process, Obatala, weary from his labor, became thirsty and unknowingly drank palm wine, which clouded his judgment. As he continued to shape humans, some of his creations became imperfect, resulting in people with disabilities or unique physical characteristics. When he realized what had happened, Obatala vowed never to consume palm wine again and became the protector of those who are born differently. This part of the myth highlights the Yoruba view on the diversity of human experiences, portraying imperfections as part of the divine design rather than flaws to be corrected.

Olokun, the Orisha of the seas, also holds an essential place in the Yoruba creation myth. According to some versions, Olokun was the original ruler of the earth and its waters before Obatala arrived. However, Olokun's dominion was confined primarily to the waters, a domain symbolizing both abundance and the unknown. When Olodumare assigned Obatala to form land and create humans, Olokun felt slighted, leading to tension between the two Orishas. Despite this tension, the earth's creation proceeded, with Olokun's domain of water remaining integral to sustaining life and reflecting the interconnectedness of all elements within Yoruba cosmology.

Esu, the messenger and trickster deity, also plays a role in maintaining balance within the universe. Although not directly involved in the act of creation, Esu's presence is critical to ensuring communication between the Orishas and humanity. As a keeper of ashe—the sacred life force that flows through everything—Esu facilitates the flow of ashe in the world, reinforcing the connection between the divine and the earthly realms. He introduces elements of unpredictability and complexity, which are integral to the Yoruba understanding of life. Without Esu, the forces of order and chaos would lack equilibrium, making him a vital, if sometimes mischievous, force in the Yoruba cosmological framework.

Each of these Orishas, with their distinct roles and attributes, contributed to the establishment of the physical and spiritual worlds in Yoruba belief. The creation myth underscores the Yoruba perception of existence as a harmonious balance between order and chaos, life and death, physical and spiritual realms. Through the actions of Olodumare, Obatala, Ogun, Olokun, and Esu, the Yoruba world was not just created but imbued with a divine purpose and structure, setting the stage for a continuous relationship between humans and the divine forces that shaped their existence.

Chapter 2: Descent of the Orishas

In Yoruba mythology, the Descent of the Orishas is a pivotal event that marks the arrival of divine beings from the heavens to the earthly realm, bridging the spiritual and physical worlds. The Orishas, powerful deities who serve as intermediaries between humanity and the supreme god Olodumare, were sent to Earth to maintain harmony, guide humans, and help shape the world according to divine will. These deities each possess distinct qualities and responsibilities, and their descent represents the Yoruba belief that divine forces are active in all aspects of existence, from the elements of nature to human morality.

According to Yoruba tradition, Olodumare observed the formless chaos of the early world and determined that it required structure, order, and care. To fulfill this vision, he summoned the Orishas, powerful spirits who would embody specific aspects of the world and guide humanity toward balance and enlightenment. Among the Orishas, Obatala was chosen as the leader due to his wisdom, purity, and creativity. Tasked with overseeing the creation of the land and forming the first humans, Obatala is often regarded as the father of humanity and the Orisha closest to Olodumare in purpose and intention. Alongside him were other Orishas, each possessing unique powers and responsibilities, creating a divine council that would guide the physical world.

Obatala descended first, equipped with sacred objects from Olodumare, including a chain made of gold to reach the earth from the heavens. This golden chain is symbolic, representing the link between the celestial and terrestrial, and reminding the Yoruba people of the ever-present connection between humanity and the divine. Obatala's initial act of descending into the unknown signified the Orishas' dedication to shaping and nurturing the earthly realm, a task that required patience, wisdom, and compassion. He was accompanied by items gifted by Olodumare, such as a bag of sand and a five-toed hen, which he used to create land upon reaching the watery, formless earth. Dropping the sand and letting the hen scratch it to spread across the waters, Obatala laid the foundation for a habitable world, bringing stability where there was once chaos.

Following Obatala, the other Orishas descended one by one, each charged with responsibilities that would enable the development and protection of life on earth. One such Orisha was Ogun, the god of iron and war. Ogun's descent introduced strength, resilience, and the transformative power of metal, providing humanity with tools essential for survival. His role as a warrior and protector embodied the spirit of discipline and bravery, and the Yoruba people associate Ogun's presence with the values of perseverance and the strength to overcome challenges. By gifting iron to humanity, Ogun ensured that they could carve paths, defend themselves, and build civilizations, demonstrating how the Orishas' descent endowed the world with practical tools as well as spiritual guidance.

Another significant figure in the Descent of the Orishas is Shango, the god of thunder, lightning, and justice. Shango's presence on Earth brought the concept of authority and righteous power, acting as a divine overseer of law, order, and balance. With his fiery energy and thunderous presence, Shango taught the importance of respect, responsibility, and accountability. His descent is a reminder that justice is an essential part of human society, and his dynamic nature inspires reverence, reminding people of the need for both strength and fairness in maintaining balance. Shango is also a protector, defending against injustices and empowering individuals to fight for truth and equity.

Oshun, the Orisha of love, beauty, and rivers, descended to bring harmony, compassion, and a deep connection to nature. As the only female Orisha in the initial group of deities, Oshun introduced qualities of nurturing, empathy, and the importance of balance in relationships. Her descent symbolized the essential need for harmony within families, communities, and the natural environment. Associated with fertility, purity, and grace, Oshun's presence on Earth is celebrated through rivers, which represent the flow of life, sustenance, and the ability to adapt to changing circumstances. She teaches the value of love and unity, reminding humanity that prosperity is linked to mutual respect and kindness.

Esu, the trickster and messenger deity, also played a critical role in the descent of the Orishas. As the keeper of ashe—the divine energy that flows through all things—Esu acted as a mediator between the Orishas and humanity, ensuring that the balance between order and chaos was maintained. Esu's role as a trickster introduces unpredictability into human life, serving as a reminder that life's path is not always straightforward. His actions can bring both fortune and mischief, challenging humans to think, adapt, and remain vigilant. Esu's descent represents the Yoruba belief in the necessity of challenges, as they provoke growth, resilience, and understanding, ensuring that life remains dynamic and multifaceted.

The Descent of the Orishas underscores the Yoruba view of the universe as a delicate interplay of forces, each represented by a deity that guides humanity in different aspects of life. Together, the Orishas not only shaped the physical world but also provided moral and spiritual frameworks for the Yoruba people, encouraging balance, respect, and reverence for the world around them. This descent created a world where the divine was ever-present, interwoven into the daily lives of humans, guiding them through challenges and triumphs alike.

Chapter 3: Obatala's Vision

In Yoruba mythology, Obatala stands as one of the most revered and significant Orishas, embodying wisdom, purity, and a vision of a balanced world. Known as the creator of humanity, Obatala's vision was to bring order, harmony, and life to the earth, acting as the divine sculptor responsible for shaping the first human beings. Olodumare, the supreme god, entrusted Obatala with the sacred mission of forming the physical bodies of humans, while Olodumare himself would grant them the breath of life. Obatala's vision of creation was rooted in patience, respect for all life, and a deep commitment to ensuring that humanity would reflect the beauty and diversity of the divine cosmos.

Obatala's journey into creation began with a descent from the heavens to the earth, carrying with him the tools and sacred materials needed to shape humanity. Equipped with a bag of clay, Obatala carefully molded human figures, breathing life into his creations through his vision of a peaceful and interconnected world. Each figure he crafted was unique, shaped with his own hands and given a form that reflected both physical and spiritual diversity. This careful, individualized approach to creation reflects the Yoruba value of honoring each being as unique and valuable, and Obatala's intent was to create a world that celebrated differences while fostering unity and balance among all life.

However, Obatala's journey was not without challenges. As he tirelessly worked to shape the earth and its inhabitants, he encountered moments of weariness and fatigue, which led him to seek relief. In one pivotal episode, Obatala, in a moment of exhaustion, consumed palm wine—a drink that, unknown to him, clouded his mind and affected his judgment. Under the influence of this drink, Obatala continued to mold human forms but made slight imperfections in some of his creations. When he sobered, he realized that some of the humans he had crafted had physical differences, marking a deviation from his original intent. Deeply remorseful for his unintended actions, Obatala vowed never again to drink palm wine and took on the role of protector of those who were born differently, seeing them as precious and unique in their own right.

Through this act, Obatala conveyed an essential lesson in Yoruba thought: that imperfections are not flaws but rather elements of diversity that enrich humanity. His compassionate response to his mistake reflects a vision of inclusivity and respect, affirming the dignity of all beings, regardless of their physical form. By embracing those with disabilities or unique characteristics, Obatala taught the Yoruba people that every individual is a sacred creation deserving of respect, love, and understanding. This vision has resonated deeply within Yoruba culture, fostering a society that values diversity as an expression of the divine's multifaceted nature.

Obatala's vision extended beyond the physical creation of humanity to the establishment of moral and ethical standards for human life. As a symbol of purity and wisdom, he exemplified patience, humility, and a peaceful approach to all matters. These qualities became the foundation of his teachings, guiding humans to live in harmony with each other and with the world around them. Obatala emphasized that anger, pride, and haste disrupt the natural order, leading to conflict and suffering. Instead, he advocated for calmness, deliberation, and compassion, inspiring the Yoruba people to emulate his virtues in their own lives. His vision was not merely of a physically balanced world but one where humanity lived in accordance with principles that promoted unity, understanding, and a deep connection to the spiritual.

In addition to his role as a creator, Obatala is also seen as a healer, bringing comfort and restoration to those who seek his guidance. His vision included a world where suffering could be alleviated through compassion and care, and he became known as the Orisha who responds to prayers for healing, both physical and emotional. Obatala's gentle and caring nature is often symbolized by the color white, representing his purity, clarity of purpose, and dedication to peace. The Yoruba associate him with coolness and calm, qualities that provide relief from life's hardships and encourage resilience in the face of adversity. His followers call upon him to restore balance when chaos threatens, and he is believed to intervene in times of discord, offering guidance that brings people back to harmony.

The animals and symbols associated with Obatala also reflect his vision and values. White animals, especially the white dove and the snail, are sacred to him, symbolizing peace, patience, and the slow, deliberate process of creation. The snail, in particular, is significant because of its cool, soothing nature, which is used in rituals to invoke Obatala's calming influence. The Yoruba people honor these animals and symbols, seeing them as representations of Obatala's vision of a world governed by patience, thoughtfulness, and balance.

Obatala's vision has had a lasting impact on the Yoruba worldview, establishing a moral framework that celebrates the interconnectedness of all beings and the value of diversity. His approach to creation, marked by care, respect, and inclusivity, serves as a guiding force within Yoruba mythology and culture, reminding people to strive for peace and harmony. Through his actions and teachings, Obatala embodies a vision of a world in which all beings are cherished as sacred expressions of the divine, where differences are embraced, and where the power of compassion unites humanity in a shared purpose.

Chapter 4: Shango, Thunder and Fire

In Yoruba mythology, Shango stands as one of the most powerful and dynamic Orishas, embodying thunder, fire, and the raw force of nature's fury. As the god of thunder and lightning, he represents justice, strength, and power, traits that make him both revered and feared by those who honor him. Shango is known for his unpredictable energy, fierce courage, and unyielding sense of justice. He is often depicted wielding a double-headed axe, symbolizing both his dominion over thunder and his role as a warrior and ruler. This weapon, called "oshe," not only signifies his ability to wield thunder and lightning but also underscores his responsibility as a divine enforcer of justice. When lightning strikes or thunder roars, it is seen as Shango's presence, a reminder of his watchful gaze and readiness to intervene when the moral order is threatened.

Shango's origin story is rich with tales of bravery, ambition, and passion, qualities that defined his life and his journey to becoming an Orisha. In many versions of the myth, Shango is described as a historical king who ruled the ancient city of Oyo, known for his unmatched strength and fiery temperament. As a ruler, he was both respected and feared, admired for his commitment to his people but often seen as impulsive and quick to anger. His reign was marked by both prosperity and conflict, and he established a legacy that was as complex as it was powerful. Shango's connection to thunder and fire reflects his intense nature and his capacity to bring both creation and destruction, qualities that the Yoruba people view as essential to maintaining balance within the universe.

According to one legend, Shango discovered his ability to command lightning and thunder when he struck his oshe against the ground, causing lightning to burst from the earth. This discovery became both his greatest asset and his most challenging responsibility, as he had to learn to control this immense power without letting it consume him. In some versions of the myth, Shango's struggle with his own strength leads to an accident in which his powers cause great destruction, resulting in the loss of many lives. This event is seen as a turning point, where Shango realizes the weight of his role and the need to channel his energy with purpose and restraint. His journey from impulsive warrior to disciplined Orisha of justice and retribution is one that reflects the Yoruba values of growth, self-awareness, and responsibility.

The fiery temperament of Shango is balanced by his commitment to justice, a quality that makes him a protector of the innocent and a punisher of those who act unjustly. He is often called upon in matters of legal disputes, personal conflicts, and moral dilemmas, as his intervention is believed to reveal the truth and restore balance. When people seek justice or feel wronged, they pray to Shango, calling on his fiery presence to uncover hidden truths and correct wrongs. He is both feared and respected for his impartiality, as he brings retribution to those who violate the moral order, regardless of their status or power. In this way, Shango is seen not just as a figure of power, but as a guardian of fairness, one who demands accountability and holds individuals to the highest standards.

Shango's association with fire and lightning also connects him to transformative energy, the force that changes and reshapes the world. Fire, in Yoruba belief, is not merely a destructive element; it is also a source of renewal and purification. Shango's fire burns away falsehoods, leaving only the truth, a process that is both feared and revered. When lightning strikes, it is believed that Shango is cleansing the land, driving away malevolent forces and purifying the earth. His fire represents the purification of the soul, a powerful and sometimes painful process that leads to growth and clarity. Shango's lightning is a reminder of his ability to strike down those who deceive or harm others, embodying the Yoruba belief that justice, while sometimes harsh, is essential for harmony in the world.

Another important aspect of Shango's character is his love for music, dance, and celebration. Despite his fierce and intense nature, Shango is also known for his joy and appreciation of life's pleasures. He is often celebrated in vibrant festivals filled with drumming, dancing, and singing, activities that are believed to honor his spirit and bring his blessings. Drums, especially, are sacred to Shango, as their sound is said to mirror the thunder he commands. His followers believe that through music and dance, they can connect with Shango's energy, channeling his strength and courage into their lives. These celebrations serve as a reminder of the balance between Shango's fierce side and his love for life, highlighting the duality of his nature as both a fearsome warrior and a deity who finds joy in the vitality of existence.

Shango's legacy is deeply embedded in Yoruba culture and extends far beyond the mythology itself. His influence can be seen in various diaspora religions, where he is celebrated and revered as a symbol of power, justice, and resilience. Followers of Shango often invoke his name when they need courage, strength, or protection, trusting that his presence will guide them through challenges and empower them to overcome obstacles. His fiery spirit and unyielding commitment to justice continue to inspire those who seek to live with integrity and purpose, embodying the Yoruba values of courage, truth, and respect for the balance of the world.

Chapter 5: Oshun: Goddess of Love and Rivers

In Yoruba mythology, Oshun is celebrated as the Orisha of love, beauty, fertility, and rivers, embodying the delicate yet powerful force of life, compassion, and the nourishing qualities of nature. She is one of the most beloved deities in the Yoruba pantheon, representing the vibrant energy of water and the deep emotional wellspring of love. Often depicted as a beautiful woman adorned with gold and radiant attire, Oshun's allure and charm symbolize her role as a goddess of attraction and harmony. She is both gentle and fierce, demonstrating that love, like water, can be both soothing and unyielding, able to sustain life and, when necessary, carve through obstacles.

Oshun's association with rivers is significant, as water represents life, renewal, and the cyclical nature of existence in Yoruba belief. Rivers are essential to communities for sustenance, and they serve as conduits for travel and communication. Just as rivers connect various lands, Oshun connects people, fostering unity and mutual respect among her followers. Her waters cleanse, heal, and restore, emphasizing her role as a nurturer and healer. Many Yoruba rituals involve offerings to rivers in her honor, symbolizing the reciprocal relationship between humans and nature. By venerating Oshun at riverbanks, her followers demonstrate respect for the environment and an understanding of their dependence on its resources.

Oshun's power is particularly evident in matters of love and fertility, where she plays a crucial role in the lives of those seeking companionship, healing, or family. Known as the goddess of sensuality and attraction, Oshun helps to form connections between people, guiding them toward relationships filled with affection, loyalty, and respect. When a person seeks love or harmony in their family life, they pray to Oshun, asking for her blessing and guidance. She represents the concept of emotional and spiritual intimacy, teaching people to cherish one another and to find joy in human connections. In the Yoruba worldview, Oshun is a reminder that love is sacred, a force that binds families and communities, creating bonds that sustain through trials and joys alike.

Oshun's role as the goddess of fertility extends beyond physical procreation to include creativity, abundance, and prosperity. She inspires artists, musicians, and writers, encouraging them to channel their emotions and passions into their work. Her influence is also seen in the agricultural realm, where she is revered as a goddess who ensures bountiful harvests. When the people seek her favor, they ask her to bless their crops and businesses, trusting that her grace will bring growth and success. Oshun's ability to bring forth life in all its forms—whether through childbirth, artistic expression, or prosperity—symbolizes the Yoruba belief in life's abundance and the endless potential for creation. Her presence in these aspects of life underscores her connection to the concept of ashe, the divine energy that flows through all things, bringing vibrancy and vitality to everything it touches.

Despite her gentle and nurturing nature, Oshun is also a fierce protector of the vulnerable, especially women and children. When people are wronged or mistreated, Oshun's anger can be as intense as a river's floodwaters. She does not tolerate cruelty or injustice, and her wrath can be swift and severe when she perceives a threat to those she loves. This duality of her character reveals the Yoruba understanding that compassion and strength are not mutually exclusive; rather, they are intertwined aspects of true love. Her fierce dedication to justice and protection reinforces her status as a goddess who stands up for the oppressed, embodying resilience and courage in the face of adversity.

One of Oshun's most famous myths speaks to her crucial role within the pantheon. It is said that when the Orishas first descended to Earth to create the world, they ignored Oshun, thinking her role unimportant. The male Orishas attempted to shape the world without her, only to fail as the land remained barren and lifeless. Realizing their mistake, they returned to Oshun and pleaded for her help. Moved by their sincerity, she agreed, pouring her waters across the earth and bringing it to life. This myth highlights the indispensable role of feminine energy in creation and emphasizes the Yoruba view that no single force can bring balance to the world alone. The Orishas learned that love, compassion, and nurturing—qualities embodied by Oshun—are as essential to creation as strength and wisdom.

Oshun's followers celebrate her in vibrant festivals filled with music, dance, and offerings of honey, oranges, and other sweet delicacies. Honey, in particular, is sacred to Oshun, symbolizing the sweetness of life and love. According to legend, there was a time when Oshun lost her sweetness due to betrayal, causing rivers to dry up and the world to lose its joy. Her devotees brought her honey as an offering, restoring her spirit and, in turn, the vitality of the land. This story illustrates the Yoruba belief that love and joy require nurturing and that even the most powerful forces of life can be vulnerable without care and respect. Her worshippers honor her through these offerings and rituals, acknowledging the delicate balance of emotions that Oshun represents and seeking to maintain harmony in their lives.

Through her association with beauty, compassion, and the nurturing qualities of water, Oshun serves as a divine guide for those seeking harmony in their lives. Her presence in Yoruba culture reminds people of the importance of balance, kindness, and the strength found in unity. She is a goddess of resilience, one who embraces both joy and sorrow, teaching that true strength lies in love's enduring power.

Chapter 6: Esu: The Trickster's Path

In Yoruba mythology, Esu is one of the most complex and fascinating Orishas, embodying the qualities of a trickster, a messenger, and a powerful mediator between the human and divine realms. Esu's role is indispensable to the Yoruba pantheon, as he represents the unpredictable forces of life, the subtle nuances of morality, and the necessity of balance in the universe. Unlike other Orishas, whose roles may be defined by clear boundaries, Esu's purpose is multifaceted and layered with contradictions. He is both revered and feared, viewed as both benevolent and mischievous, yet his actions, however perplexing, serve a vital function in maintaining cosmic equilibrium. Esu is often called upon when clarity or resolution is needed, as he can unveil hidden truths or reveal paths that others might overlook.

Esu's appearance and symbols reflect his unique position in the pantheon. He is often depicted with a distinctive red and black color scheme, signifying both life and death, light and darkness, order and chaos. These opposing elements illustrate his dual nature as a figure who can sway the balance between good and evil, a reminder that life is filled with contradictions that must coexist to create harmony. Esu often carries a staff or stone that represents his role as a messenger, traveling between the earthly and divine realms to convey the words and will of Olodumare, the supreme god. He serves as the bridge between humans and other Orishas, delivering offerings, prayers, and messages. In this role, Esu possesses ashe, the divine force that connects all things, enabling him to influence events, sway decisions, and affect the outcomes of both mundane and extraordinary situations.

As the trickster, Esu introduces uncertainty, challenging humans to question their assumptions, confront their flaws, and face the unexpected twists of life. He has the power to alter circumstances in ways that seem chaotic or unpredictable, yet his actions often reveal deeper lessons about human nature and morality. Esu is known for his cleverness and wit, frequently using these qualities to test people's integrity, patience, and intentions. For example, in many Yoruba tales, Esu appears to provoke individuals by creating situations that expose their hidden motives or bring their weaknesses to light. In these stories, he might present two travelers with the same choice, leading each to act in ways that reveal their true character. In this way, Esu becomes not only a trickster but a mirror, reflecting the innermost qualities of those he encounters and urging them to learn from their own behavior.

One of the key aspects of Esu's nature is his role in challenging the established order, illustrating that growth often comes through disruption and transformation. Esu is not bound by conventional morality; instead, he embodies the idea that there is no growth without challenge, no wisdom without experience. His actions may sometimes appear disruptive, but they encourage people to adapt, to rethink, and to develop resilience. Esu's influence is especially felt in situations of conflict or decision-making, as he reveals the hidden dimensions of a problem and forces individuals to look beyond their immediate perceptions. He is known to cause confusion, yet this confusion often prompts people to search for clarity within themselves, finding solutions and insights they might not have otherwise discovered.

In addition to his role as a trickster, Esu is also a fierce protector of truth and justice. He detests hypocrisy, deception, and dishonesty, and he punishes those who act with malice or deceit. Esu's punishments can be swift and unexpected, as he has the ability to shift fortunes quickly, rewarding the honest and humbling the deceitful. In this sense, Esu is seen as a moral compass, albeit an unconventional one, reminding people that integrity is paramount and that their actions have consequences. When individuals act with sincerity and respect, Esu often supports their endeavors, clearing obstacles from their path and granting them success. However, those who act dishonestly or harmfully must contend with Esu's unpredictable justice, often learning that deception cannot remain hidden for long.

Esu's role as a messenger extends to his capacity to facilitate communication and understanding. He is often called upon to settle disputes, mediate conflicts, and restore balance when relationships are strained. Through his wisdom and insight, Esu helps individuals and communities navigate complex issues, offering guidance that fosters unity and mutual respect. His influence is particularly revered in divination practices, where he helps interpret messages from the spiritual world. Diviners and priests rely on Esu to ensure that they correctly understand the will of the Orishas and convey it accurately to the people. Esu's presence in these rituals underscores his role as the bridge between the earthly and divine realms, a guide who helps humanity navigate the mysteries of existence with insight and humility. While Esu's actions may be perplexing or even disruptive, he is ultimately a force for balance and understanding. His trickery and challenges serve as vital reminders that life is not a straightforward path but a series of interconnected events, decisions, and consequences. The Yoruba understand that Esu's influence is necessary for growth and enlightenment, as he urges them to confront their limitations, embrace the unknown, and strive for wisdom through experience. By embracing Esu, they accept life's uncertainties and complexities, acknowledging that the journey toward truth often involves navigating through shadows, overcoming obstacles, and seeking clarity amidst confusion. In every twist and turn, Esu is there, guiding them on the trickster's path, a path that teaches resilience, insight, and the unbreakable link between humanity and the divine.

Chapter 7: Oya: Queen of Winds and Change

In Yoruba mythology, Oya is the powerful Orisha of winds, storms, and transformation, often revered as the Queen of Change. As a goddess of unpredictable forces, she embodies the volatile, life-altering power of wind and storm, representing the natural forces that tear down the old to make way for the new. Oya's presence signifies both destruction and renewal, as she removes what is stagnant, allowing for growth and transformation. Her influence is far-reaching, touching both the physical world and the emotional lives of those who worship her. Known for her courage and intensity, she is celebrated as a warrior deity, standing strong in the face of adversity and inspiring her followers to embrace change with the same strength and resilience.

Oya's association with wind is particularly significant, as wind represents movement, energy, and unseen forces that shape the world. In the Yoruba worldview, the wind is a reminder of the invisible currents that affect people's lives, influencing events and bringing sudden changes. Oya, as the master of these winds, controls the flow of life's transitions, reminding her followers that change is inevitable and necessary. Her winds are powerful enough to uproot trees and reshape landscapes, demonstrating her ability to alter the course of events dramatically. When Oya is invoked, people understand that a transformation is imminent, as she clears away obstacles and creates space for new beginnings. The Yoruba often see her as a force that brings both destruction and opportunity, as her storms sweep away the old and open the path to renewal.

As a warrior goddess, Oya is also deeply connected to themes of courage and strength. She is often depicted wielding a machete or sword, ready to fight against injustice or to protect those who cannot protect themselves. This image of Oya as a fierce warrior reflects her role as a protector and a champion of those in need. Her strength is not limited to physical battles; she is equally formidable in the face of emotional and spiritual struggles. When individuals call upon Oya, they seek her bravery and fortitude, asking her to help them face challenges and to cut through the obstacles that stand in their way. She teaches that true strength lies in the willingness to confront difficulties head-on, even when the path forward is uncertain or perilous. Her worshippers look to her as a source of empowerment, drawing upon her courage to embrace change and navigate the storms of life.

Oya's transformative power also extends to the realms of birth, death, and rebirth, as she governs the cycle of life and the transitions between these stages. In Yoruba belief, she is closely associated with cemeteries and the passage between the physical and spiritual worlds. As a guardian of the dead, Oya oversees the journey of the soul, guiding it through the threshold between life and the afterlife. Her connection to cemeteries underscores her role in transformation and renewal, as death is viewed not as an end but as a transition to a new form of existence. Oya's presence at this critical juncture signifies her ability to shepherd souls from one state to another, and her followers honor her as a protector of both the living and the dead. Through her guidance, they are reminded that endings are often beginnings in disguise, and that change, however difficult, is part of the natural order.

Another important aspect of Oya's character is her association with lightning, which, like the wind, represents sudden and impactful change. Lightning is a swift and powerful force that can illuminate and destroy in an instant, symbolizing Oya's capacity to bring clarity and transformation through intense, sometimes unsettling, events. She is the spark that ignites change, the force that reveals hidden truths and dispels illusions. Lightning's brilliance mirrors Oya's ability to bring sudden insight or to catalyze an awakening, often through events that force individuals to re-evaluate their lives. Her lightning serves as both a warning and a blessing, shaking people out of complacency and encouraging them to embrace their own power to effect change.

Oya's relationship with other Orishas, particularly Shango, the god of thunder, further highlights her dynamic role within the Yoruba pantheon. She is often depicted as Shango's consort, and their connection reflects the balance between storm and fire, wind and thunder. Together, they embody the dual forces of destruction and creation, representing the power to break down and rebuild. While Shango's thunder brings strength and authority, Oya's winds bring flexibility and adaptability. This partnership illustrates the Yoruba understanding that change requires both intensity and fluidity, both force and freedom. Through their combined influence, Oya and Shango teach that true transformation is a blend of destruction and renewal, an intricate dance between forces that seem opposed but are, in reality, interdependent.

Oya's followers honor her in ceremonies that celebrate both her fierce strength and her nurturing side. They offer her copper, red and purple cloth, and fresh fruits, symbols of her energy and vitality. These offerings acknowledge her dual nature as a goddess of both storm and life, chaos and creation. During festivals dedicated to her, devotees dance and sing, invoking her spirit to enter their lives and guide them through personal transformations. The energy of these rituals reflects Oya's presence: vibrant, powerful, and uncontainable. Her devotees believe that by embracing Oya's spirit, they can find the courage to face their fears and the strength to embrace change, knowing that she is with them as they navigate life's unpredictable paths.

Through her roles as a warrior, protector, and guide, Oya teaches the importance of embracing change as an integral part of existence. She reminds her followers that life's storms are not obstacles but pathways to growth, that every ending holds the promise of renewal, and that even the most turbulent transformations are essential for personal and spiritual evolution. In the winds that sweep through the earth, the lightning that illuminates the night, and the transitions that shape human lives, Oya's presence endures as the ultimate symbol of strength, courage, and transformation.

Chapter 8: Ogun: The Forge of War and Creation

In Yoruba mythology, Ogun is the powerful Orisha of iron, war, and creation, embodying the resilience, determination, and transformative force of metal. Known as the god of the forge, he is deeply revered as a creator and protector, a figure who has both constructive and destructive powers. Ogun's essence is found in iron and steel, materials that have shaped human civilization through tools, weapons, and structures. The Yoruba people view him as the spirit within these metals, a deity who has given humanity the means to build, to defend, and to innovate. His gifts are crucial for survival and progress, reflecting the duality of his role as both a fierce warrior and a skilled craftsman. He is also called upon in times of conflict and struggle, trusted for his strength and his unwavering sense of justice.

Ogun's origin story is rooted in his journey to bring the knowledge of ironworking to humanity. According to Yoruba tradition, he descended from the heavens with iron tools and the knowledge of metalwork, providing humans with the skills to create tools that would transform their world. As he descended from the heavens, he carried a machete, symbolizing his power to clear paths and conquer the wilderness, and a hammer, representing his ability to shape and forge materials into useful forms. In his hands, iron becomes both a weapon and a tool, emphasizing Ogun's role as a force of duality who brings forth both destruction and creation. He is not merely a warrior but also an inventor, an artist who sculpts the raw potential of metal into something purposeful. Through him, the Yoruba people learned that iron could serve as a foundation for civilization, a means of survival, and a testament to human ingenuity.

Ogun's presence is especially revered in war, where he embodies the spirit of courage, strength, and resilience. In battle, he is the fearless warrior who leads his followers, bestowing them with bravery and the indomitable will to overcome adversity. As a god of war, he is relentless, symbolizing the strength to confront challenges head-on and to fight for one's beliefs and values. His followers believe that Ogun stands with them in times of conflict, lending his strength to those who seek justice and protection. The Yoruba honor him by invoking his name before entering battle, calling upon his power to grant them victory and defend them from harm. His nature is fierce and unyielding, demanding respect and commitment from those who call upon him, and he expects his followers to approach their struggles with the same courage and determination that he embodies.

Despite his fierce nature in war, Ogun's influence extends beyond combat; he is equally known as the Orisha of creation, innovation, and progress. The tools he provides are essential for shaping the physical world, building communities, and creating structures that support human life. The Yoruba see him in the blacksmith's forge, where raw metal is transformed through heat and pressure into something new and useful. In this context, Ogun is a figure of patience and focus, overseeing the slow, deliberate process that turns iron ore into tools, weapons, and art.

He teaches that creation requires endurance, that one must be willing to withstand the fires of transformation to achieve something worthwhile. Ogun's forge is both a literal and symbolic space of change, where the old is broken down, and the new emerges through skill and labor.

Ogun's association with metal also makes him a deity of integrity and justice. Iron, strong and unyielding, represents truth and moral fortitude, qualities that Ogun upholds as sacred. He detests deceit and dishonesty, and those who act with treachery or malice risk invoking his wrath. The Yoruba believe that Ogun rewards those who are honorable and straightforward, and that he has little tolerance for corruption or cowardice. His judgments are swift and uncompromising, and his sense of justice is one that upholds integrity and transparency. For this reason, people often call upon Ogun to witness oaths and agreements, as his presence is believed to enforce honesty and hold individuals accountable. His sense of justice aligns with his role as a god of war, as both demand courage, responsibility, and an unwavering commitment to truth.

Ogun's followers honor him through rituals involving iron objects, sacrifices, and offerings that reflect his fierce and resilient nature. Blacksmiths, soldiers, and hunters especially revere Ogun, recognizing him as the source of their strength and the protector of their crafts. His shrines are often adorned with iron tools and weapons, symbolizing his mastery over metal and his role as the father of all who work with iron. During ceremonies, his devotees perform dances, wielding machetes or spears to symbolize his power and their own connection to his enduring strength. These rituals reinforce Ogun's teachings of resilience, focus, and the importance of hard work, encouraging his followers to embrace life's challenges and to create with purpose and dedication.

Ogun's presence in Yoruba culture and beyond extends into various forms of expression, including art, music, and craftsmanship, all of which celebrate his contributions to humanity. His legacy lives on in the tools and technologies that continue to shape society, from agricultural implements to modern machinery. Ogun's essence is seen in every creation that comes from raw materials shaped by human hands, as his spirit inspires innovation and the courage to break new ground. His story teaches that creation and destruction are two sides of the same coin, that progress often requires sacrifice, and that strength lies in the ability to forge ahead, no matter the obstacles. As the god of iron, war, and creation, Ogun's influence endures, guiding those who seek strength, justice, and the power to shape their own destinies.

Chapter 9: Healing and Divination

In Yoruba mythology, healing and divination are sacred practices deeply interwoven with the spiritual fabric of the culture, regarded as essential means for connecting with the divine and maintaining balance in the physical and spiritual worlds. These practices are not merely acts of physical restoration or fortune-telling; they represent a profound system of communication with the Orishas, where each ritual, plant, and spoken word carries sacred meaning. Through healing and divination, the Yoruba people seek guidance, understanding, and alignment with their higher purpose, viewing health and insight as intertwined states of harmony between the body, mind, and soul. The Orishas play an integral role in both practices, serving as intermediaries who help humans achieve well-being and clarity.

Central to Yoruba healing is the belief that illness or misfortune often results from an imbalance between the individual and their spiritual environment. This imbalance can arise from a range of causes, such as unresolved conflicts, broken taboos, or neglected ancestral obligations. As such, Yoruba healers, often called *babalawos* (priests) or *iyalawos* (priestesses), approach illness from a holistic perspective, seeking to understand the deeper issues that may be affecting the individual. These healers are highly respected figures, skilled in herbal medicine, spiritual knowledge, and the rituals necessary to restore balance. They draw upon an extensive array of medicinal plants, minerals, and natural elements, each selected for its specific healing properties, as well as its symbolic resonance within Yoruba cosmology. These elements are combined with prayer, incantations, and offerings to invoke the blessing of Orishas like Osanyin, the Orisha of herbal knowledge, who governs the secrets of nature's healing potential.

Osanyin, often depicted as a figure who commands all the plants and trees, is essential to Yoruba healing. His knowledge of every plant's properties and his power over vegetation make him a central figure for healers who rely on his wisdom to select the right combinations of herbs for various ailments. According to legend, Osanyin once withheld the knowledge of healing plants from other Orishas, choosing to keep his secrets close. However, when his power was eventually shared, the Yoruba people received access to the boundless healing resources of the earth. Today, Osanyin is invoked whenever herbs are gathered for healing, as his blessing is thought to activate the plants' spiritual properties, transforming them into vessels of divine energy that can restore harmony within the body.

Divination, another cornerstone of Yoruba spiritual practice, works alongside healing to offer insight and guidance on the path to health and understanding. The Yoruba people believe that the future is not fixed but shaped by the choices individuals make and the guidance they receive from the Orishas. Divination provides a way to communicate with the spiritual realm, allowing humans to uncover their destinies, seek advice, and find answers to pressing questions. The most respected method of divination in Yoruba culture is *Ifá*, a complex system presided over by Orunmila, the Orisha of wisdom and prophecy. Orunmila is said to possess knowledge of all destinies, and through Ifá, he reveals the paths that individuals must follow to achieve their purpose and avoid misfortune.

In the Ifá divination process, a babalawo interprets patterns formed by casting palm nuts or cowrie shells, each pattern corresponding to a specific verse or proverb that reveals insight into the question at hand. These verses are part of an extensive oral tradition containing thousands of sacred texts, each with layers of meaning and advice. The babalawo's role is to interpret these signs accurately and provide guidance that aligns the individual with their divine path. Divination is not limited to fortune-telling; it is a transformative experience that helps individuals understand their current challenges, strengths, and relationships with the Orishas. Through Ifá, people receive advice on everything from personal conflicts to major life decisions, with Orunmila's wisdom guiding them toward outcomes that enhance their spiritual and earthly well-being.

Healing and divination often intersect, as the information obtained through divination may reveal the root causes of illness or misfortune, providing a foundation for the healing process. For instance, a babalawo might use Ifá to determine whether an illness is due to natural causes or spiritual disruption, guiding the healer to treat the individual accordingly. Sometimes, the divination will prescribe specific offerings or rituals to appease an Orisha or address an imbalance. These offerings can include food, objects, or acts of service that demonstrate respect and reverence for the divine. By engaging in these rituals, individuals participate in a reciprocal relationship with the Orishas, acknowledging the interconnectedness of all aspects of life and seeking to restore harmony through gratitude and respect.

Divination and healing also reflect the Yoruba understanding of destiny and free will. While divination reveals possible outcomes, individuals must choose how to act on this knowledge, a choice that allows them to actively shape their destiny. Healing, too, requires active participation; it is not a passive process but one that calls for commitment to one's own well-being and alignment with the divine. Through both practices, the Yoruba people learn that they are not alone in their struggles; they are supported by the wisdom and compassion of the Orishas, who stand ready to assist them on their journey toward health, knowledge, and spiritual fulfillment.

For the Yoruba, healing and divination are sacred gifts, pathways to a life in harmony with the self, the community, and the divine. These practices reinforce the Yoruba belief in ashe, the life force that flows through everything, linking humans, nature, and the Orishas in a continuous cycle of influence and interdependence. Through healing, they restore ashe within the body, while through divination, they align ashe with their purpose and destiny, strengthening their connection to the spiritual world and reinforcing their commitment to a life of balance, integrity, and fulfillment.

Chapter 10: The Eternal Legacy of the Orishas

The Orishas of Yoruba mythology have left an enduring legacy that transcends time, borders, and cultural boundaries, continuing to shape the lives and spirituality of millions across the world. Rooted in the West African Yoruba culture, the Orishas are divine beings representing various forces of nature, embodying qualities and virtues that resonate deeply with the human experience. Each Orisha carries unique attributes and stories, personifying universal elements such as courage, love, justice, wisdom, and transformation. Over centuries, the Orishas have woven their essence into the hearts of the Yoruba people and, through the transatlantic diaspora, into the wider world. Today, their influence reaches beyond religion, touching art, music, literature, and cultural identity in profound ways.

The journey of the Orishas across the globe is one marked by resilience and adaptation. When enslaved Africans were forcibly brought to the Americas, they carried with them the spiritual traditions of their homeland, including the reverence for the Orishas. In new and often hostile environments, these beliefs served as a source of strength, unity, and resistance. Under oppressive conditions, the enslaved communities found ways to preserve their traditions, incorporating the Orishas into their daily lives despite attempts to erase their culture. To survive and adapt, the Yoruba people merged their beliefs with those of the dominant colonial religions, creating syncretic practices that allowed the Orishas to flourish in disguise. This syncretism led to the development of Afro-Caribbean religions such as Santería in Cuba, Candomblé in Brazil, and Vodou in Haiti, where the Orishas were blended with Catholic saints to ensure their survival.

Through these syncretic practices, the Orishas maintained their core attributes, embodying the same virtues and domains they held in Yoruba tradition. Shango, the Orisha of thunder, retained his role as a powerful figure of justice and protection; Oshun, goddess of rivers and love, continued to inspire compassion and healing; and Ogun, god of iron and war, remained a symbol of strength, labor, and resilience. These qualities found new meaning in the Americas, where the descendants of enslaved Africans drew upon the Orishas as symbols of hope, endurance, and liberation. The Orishas became not only gods but cultural ancestors, sources of pride, and emblems of survival against centuries of oppression. In the Caribbean, Brazil, and beyond, festivals, music, and dances honoring the Orishas continue to be vibrant expressions of cultural identity, echoing the resilience of the Yoruba people and their determination to keep their heritage alive.

Beyond the Afro-Caribbean and Afro-Latin communities, the Orishas have also captured the interest of those seeking spirituality that connects them to nature, community, and inner strength. As modern societies look for meaning beyond materialism and individualism, many people find inspiration in the teachings and symbolism of the Orishas. In contemporary times, these deities represent more than myth; they embody timeless principles of balance, integrity, and courage. The Orishas' connection to natural elements, such as rivers, forests, and skies, resonates with those who seek harmony with the environment. This resonance is particularly powerful in a world grappling with ecological challenges, as the Orishas remind people of the sacred relationship between humanity and the Earth.

The Orishas also continue to inspire art, literature, and music, leaving their mark on popular culture worldwide. Artists and writers draw upon the rich stories of the Orishas, finding in them powerful metaphors for personal and social transformation. The character of Oshun, with her associations with love and resilience, appears in poetry and visual art as a symbol of empowerment and femininity. Shango's fierce image, representing justice and authority, inspires narratives of defiance against oppression. In music, rhythms and beats inspired by traditional Yoruba drumming are woven into genres such as jazz, salsa, and hip-hop, carrying the spirit of the Orishas through sound and movement. Through these creative expressions, the Orishas live on, continuing to shape the identities and aspirations of people across generations.

In religious practice, the Orishas provide a deeply personal connection to the divine, allowing followers to engage with gods who understand their joys and sorrows, their strengths and weaknesses. Each Orisha has a story that reflects some aspect of the human condition, making them relatable figures to those who seek spiritual guidance. The stories of the Orishas, with their struggles, triumphs, and lessons, offer insights that help individuals navigate their own lives. Devotees build altars, give offerings, and engage in ceremonies, not only to seek blessings but to feel connected to a tradition that emphasizes community, respect, and the pursuit of a balanced life. The Orishas remind their followers of the interconnectedness of all beings, the cycles of growth and renewal, and the importance of living in harmony with oneself and others.

As the Orishas continue to influence new generations, their teachings offer pathways to resilience, self-discovery, and spiritual connection. Through rituals, storytelling, and community gatherings, their legacy endures, resonating with those who feel drawn to a spirituality that honors both individual identity and collective unity. The values they embody—such as strength in adversity, compassion, integrity, and courage—remain as relevant today as they were centuries ago. In a world that constantly shifts and changes, the Orishas serve as steadfast guides, helping people navigate the complexities of modern life while staying rooted in timeless wisdom. Through the enduring legacy of the Orishas, the Yoruba tradition lives on, demonstrating the profound power of spirituality to inspire, uplift, and sustain across generations and cultures.

BOOK 2
DOGON MYTHOLOGY
STARS AND SPIRITS: THE MYSTICAL WORLD OF DOGON MYTHOLOGY
SAMUEL SHEPHERD

Chapter 1: In the Beginning of Time

In Dogon mythology, the creation of the universe is a profound narrative that reveals the Dogon people's intricate understanding of the cosmos and the forces that govern it. This mythology, originating with the Dogon people of Mali in West Africa, describes a universe shaped by balance, duality, and the interplay of natural elements. The story begins with Amma, the supreme god, who exists alone in the vast, silent emptiness before creation. Amma is depicted as both male and female, embodying all potential and completeness within. The Dogon believe that before anything could take shape, Amma first had to bring forth matter from his own being, a process that initiated the unfolding of space, time, and life.

Amma's first act of creation was to form a large, egg-like structure that contained the entire universe in its primordial state. This cosmic egg held within it the seeds of everything that would eventually emerge—light, darkness, stars, planets, and even the souls of living beings. According to Dogon cosmology, the universe began as this closed, pulsating egg, full of latent energy and possibility. Within this egg, Amma introduced twin spirals, symbolizing the duality of all things. This duality is central to Dogon philosophy, which emphasizes the importance of balance between opposing forces, such as male and female, light and darkness, or earth and sky. As the cosmic egg began to expand, these forces separated, marking the beginning of differentiation and the unfolding of creation.

The most important figures to emerge from Amma's act of creation were the Nommo, amphibious beings that are considered the ancestors of all life. The Nommo were born in pairs, each embodying a combination of male and female energy, reflecting the Dogon belief in the unity of opposites. The Nommo were sent to Earth to serve as both creators and teachers, guiding humanity toward harmony with the natural world and helping to establish the fundamental principles of Dogon life. They are often depicted as serpent-like beings, symbolizing both the fluidity and adaptability of water, an element essential to life. The Nommo's descent to Earth marks the beginning of life and the unfolding of the Dogon people's sacred knowledge, which encompasses astronomy, agriculture, and spiritual practices.

Amma's creation of the Nommo was not without challenges, as Dogon mythology also tells of a rebellious entity known as Yurugu, or the Pale Fox. Yurugu is depicted as an impulsive being who defied Amma's order and disrupted the harmony of creation. According to the Dogon, Yurugu separated himself prematurely from the cosmic egg, embodying chaos and incompletion. His rebellion introduced imperfection into the universe, creating imbalance and sparking a cosmic struggle between order and disorder. Yurugu's disruptive energy is viewed as a necessary aspect of the world, representing the unpredictability and imperfections that are inherent to life. The Dogon believe that through this disruption, Amma allowed space for growth, transformation, and the pursuit of knowledge, as humans are continually challenged to restore harmony in an imperfect world. To counteract Yurugu's influence and restore order, Amma sent the Nommo to teach humanity the principles of balance, unity, and cosmic awareness. The Nommo introduced language, knowledge of agriculture, and sacred rituals, all of which helped the Dogon cultivate a deep connection to the cycles of nature and the stars. Dogon mythology places special emphasis on the Sirius star system, which the Nommo are said to have come from. The Dogon hold that the Sirius stars—particularly Sirius B, a star invisible to the naked eye—have a profound connection to the Nommo's journey and influence on Earth. This astronomical knowledge, passed down through generations, is an essential aspect of Dogon spirituality, revealing their understanding of a vast, interconnected cosmos. The Nommo's teachings encourage the Dogon to look beyond the earthly plane and see their lives as part of a larger, cosmic order.

Dogon rituals and ceremonies honor Amma, the Nommo, and the cosmic forces that shape their existence, reinforcing their reverence for the balance between order and chaos. One of the most important rituals is the Sigui, a complex, multi-year ceremony held every sixty years to celebrate the connection between the Earth and the Sirius star system. The Sigui is a time of renewal and reflection, during which the Dogon people reenact the creation story and reaffirm their commitment to harmony and cosmic alignment. The ceremony reflects the Dogon understanding of time as cyclical rather than linear, echoing the movements of celestial bodies and the ongoing process of creation, destruction, and renewal.

Through their creation myth, the Dogon people express a worldview that places humanity within a network of cosmic relationships, each governed by natural rhythms and sacred principles. The myth teaches that every aspect of existence, from the stars to the water to the human spirit, is interrelated and constantly influenced by the forces that began with Amma's first act of creation. The Dogon see themselves as stewards of this cosmic order, tasked with maintaining balance and understanding their role within the broader universe. The mythology encourages respect for all life and a recognition of the unseen forces that shape their world, as the Dogon strive to live in harmony with the legacy of the Nommo and the teachings imparted from the time of creation.

The Dogon creation myth not only provides an explanation for the origins of the universe but also serves as a moral framework, guiding individuals toward balance, respect, and cosmic awareness. Through rituals, stories, and observances, the Dogon continue to honor the beginning of time, viewing creation as an ongoing, sacred process that reflects the dual nature of the universe and the ever-present connection between the physical and spiritual worlds. In their reverence for the Nommo and Amma, the Dogon maintain a worldview where humanity and the cosmos are intimately bound, each life a reflection of the primordial unity that began at the dawn of creation.

Chapter 2: Amma, the Supreme Creator

In Dogon mythology, Amma stands as the supreme creator, the source of all existence and the force that governs the universe's balance and order. Amma's nature is complex and multifaceted, embodying both male and female aspects, which reflect the Dogon understanding of duality and unity within creation. The Dogon people regard Amma as both omnipotent and omnipresent, a deity whose presence infuses every aspect of life and the cosmos. Before time began, Amma existed alone in an unchanging, formless void. In this vast emptiness, Amma held the potential of creation within, a force waiting to emerge and manifest into the physical and spiritual realms. This potential, embodied in Amma, contains all opposites—light and darkness, chaos and order, male and female—waiting for the moment of creation to unfold.

The Dogon believe that Amma's initial act of creation involved shaping a great cosmic egg, a vessel that would hold the essence of the universe. Within this egg lay all the elements that would later form the cosmos, from stars and planets to the spirits of living beings. This cosmic egg was a microcosm of creation itself, containing within it the seeds of life, consciousness, and all forms of matter. The egg was bound together by a vital force, a divine energy that Amma imbued into it, ensuring that everything within it was interconnected and that each part had a purpose within the grand design of the universe. The Dogon people see this cosmic egg as the birthplace of existence, a sacred and foundational symbol representing the unity of all things within the world Amma created.

Amma's creation of the cosmic egg involved the careful balancing of opposites, a theme that permeates Dogon cosmology and mythology. The Dogon emphasize that Amma crafted the universe with a precise equilibrium between male and female forces, between darkness and light, to ensure harmony and continuity. These elements are not separate or conflicting; rather, they are interconnected aspects of a unified whole. Amma's balance between dualities is seen as the underlying principle of existence, guiding the cycles of birth, death, and renewal that define the natural and spiritual worlds. This balance is not static but a dynamic process that Amma continuously oversees, intervening when the natural order is threatened and adjusting the universe as needed.

One of Amma's most significant creations was the Nommo, a set of twin beings born from Amma's act of bringing life into the universe. The Nommo are amphibious, water-dwelling beings who embody both human and divine qualities, serving as the first ancestors of humankind. They are revered as messengers and teachers, guiding humanity and imparting sacred knowledge about the workings of the cosmos. Each pair of Nommo represents the duality and unity Amma intended for all creation, symbolizing the interconnectedness between the physical and spiritual worlds. Through the Nommo, Amma granted humans the wisdom to live in harmony with nature, to honor the natural cycles, and to maintain the cosmic balance. The Dogon people view the Nommo as living embodiments of Amma's will, sent to Earth to help humanity understand their place within the larger universe.

In Dogon mythology, Amma's act of creation was not without disruption. A rebellious figure named Yurugu, or the Pale Fox, arose, embodying chaos and imperfection. Yurugu attempted to separate himself from Amma's cosmic egg prematurely, disrupting the delicate balance that Amma had intended. This act introduced disorder into the world, creating challenges that would shape human experience. Yurugu's rebellion is often interpreted as a metaphor for the imperfections inherent in life, reflecting the Dogon understanding that struggle and disharmony are natural parts of the world. Amma, however, did not eliminate Yurugu's influence. Instead, Amma incorporated Yurugu's chaotic energy into the cosmic order, using it as a counterbalance to the harmony embodied by the Nommo. This balance between order and chaos, symbolized by the contrasting forces of the Nommo and Yurugu, underscores the Dogon belief that both are essential to creation, each playing a role in the dynamic, evolving universe.

Amma's relationship with the Dogon people extends beyond creation. Amma is not a distant deity but an active presence in the world, guiding and overseeing the cycles of life, death, and rebirth. Through rituals, ceremonies, and offerings, the Dogon honor Amma and seek divine favor and guidance. These acts of devotion are ways for the Dogon to align themselves with Amma's vision for the universe, demonstrating their commitment to upholding the balance that Amma established. During these rituals, the Dogon invoke Amma's blessing for fertility, prosperity, and protection, reinforcing their connection to the divine and acknowledging Amma's role as the sustainer of life and cosmic order.

Amma's influence also extends to the realm of knowledge and understanding. Through divination practices and teachings passed down from the Nommo, the Dogon people continually seek to deepen their understanding of the universe, believing that true wisdom is found in aligning oneself with Amma's cosmic plan. This pursuit of knowledge is viewed as a sacred duty, a way for humanity to fulfill its role within the grand design. Amma's teachings encourage the Dogon to respect all forms of life, to act with integrity, and to recognize the interconnectedness of all beings. These values, embedded in Amma's creation of the universe, shape Dogon ethics and worldview, providing a foundation for both individual behavior and communal life.

In Dogon mythology, Amma's legacy is one of balance, unity, and ongoing creation. Amma's actions at the beginning of time continue to echo through the cycles of nature and the lives of the Dogon people, who see themselves as custodians of the sacred order established by their creator. Through their reverence for Amma, the Dogon maintain a deep connection to the divine source of existence, drawing strength, wisdom, and purpose from the understanding that they are part of a cosmic order that began with Amma's first act of creation.

Chapter 3: The Birth of the Nommo

In Dogon mythology, the Nommo are central figures of creation, beings of profound importance who embody the divine balance, wisdom, and order intended by Amma, the supreme creator. The story of the Nommo's birth is not only the beginning of life on Earth but also the introduction of knowledge, language, and order to humanity. Amma, who exists as both creator and sustainer of the universe, brought the Nommo into existence as an answer to the initial chaos and imperfection that emerged from creation. These beings are often depicted as amphibious, with both human and serpent-like qualities, symbolizing their adaptability and the seamless link between the spiritual and physical realms. Born from Amma's cosmic egg, the Nommo were not only created to bring life but to guide it, serving as the first ancestors and teachers to the Dogon people.

The Nommo are described in Dogon mythology as twin beings, a reflection of Amma's emphasis on duality and balance. This dual nature is intrinsic to their identity, representing the harmony of opposites that Amma wove into the fabric of the universe. The Dogon believe that the cosmic egg from which the Nommo were born contained all elements in a state of potential, and that the Nommo embodied these elements, each pair symbolizing male and female, day and night, life and death. This duality was essential for creating a stable, balanced world, as it mirrored the interconnected nature of all things. The Nommo's twin nature reinforced the Dogon's understanding that life's true essence lies in balance, where opposing forces do not compete but coexist, enhancing and complementing one another.

After their birth, the Nommo descended to Earth with the mission to establish order and teach humanity the sacred principles necessary to maintain harmony in a world that contained both creative and destructive forces. As they descended, they carried with them the knowledge of agriculture, astronomy, and the spiritual practices that would guide the Dogon people. Their arrival marked the beginning of civilization, a transition from chaos to structure, from silence to language. The Nommo, as divine teachers, introduced the Dogon to language and communication, tools that would not only connect people with each other but also allow them to express reverence for the divine. Through language, the Nommo taught the Dogon to name and understand the world around them, making sense of the stars, the earth, and the complex interrelations of nature.

One of the most significant teachings the Nommo brought was the knowledge of the Sirius star system, particularly the star Sirius B, which holds an essential place in Dogon cosmology. The Nommo are believed to have originated from this star system, descending to Earth with wisdom from a realm beyond the visible. The Dogon people, through the teachings of the Nommo, possessed intricate knowledge about Sirius B, even knowing of its existence before modern telescopes could confirm it. This knowledge, transmitted through generations, reflects the Nommo's role as cosmic messengers, connecting the Dogon to a broader universe and instilling a sense of awe and interconnectedness that extends far beyond the visible stars.

In addition to knowledge of the cosmos, the Nommo brought with them the sacred rhythms and rituals that would become the foundation of Dogon spirituality. These rituals were designed to honor Amma, the supreme creator, and to align the Dogon people with the natural rhythms of life and the universe. By teaching them these practices, the Nommo ensured that the Dogon would maintain a spiritual connection to the cosmos and to their ancestors. Each ceremony, dance, and song holds symbolic meaning, celebrating the cycles of life and paying homage to the divine. The Nommo's presence is invoked during these rituals, serving as a bridge between the earthly and spiritual realms and reminding the Dogon of their connection to the forces that govern all existence.

The Nommo's teachings extended beyond ritual and astronomy to the realms of ethics and social harmony. They instructed the Dogon in the principles of balance, respect, and communal responsibility, values that became deeply embedded in Dogon culture. The Nommo taught that life was a shared journey, that individuals were responsible for both their own well-being and the well-being of others. This emphasis on community and mutual support reinforced the Dogon's understanding of interconnectedness, a belief that every action has a ripple effect, impacting not only the individual but the whole. By following the principles taught by the Nommo, the Dogon learned to live in harmony with each other, with nature, and with the spiritual forces that shaped their world.

The Dogon also credit the Nommo with introducing the knowledge of water as a sacred and life-giving force. Water, the element associated with the Nommo, symbolizes renewal, adaptability, and the flow of life. The Nommo's amphibious nature reflects this association, as they embody the qualities of water in their teachings and existence. The Dogon view water as a bridge between the spiritual and physical worlds, a source of sustenance that sustains both body and spirit. Through the Nommo, water became more than a physical necessity; it became a symbol of the divine flow that connects all things, a reminder of life's continuous cycle and the need to honor and protect this essential resource.

The legacy of the Nommo, as the first beings born from Amma's cosmic egg, continues to shape Dogon spirituality, rituals, and worldview. As cosmic ancestors, the Nommo left a lasting imprint on the Dogon, who see themselves as custodians of the knowledge imparted by these divine beings. Through stories, ceremonies, and everyday practices, the Dogon people honor the Nommo's teachings, maintaining a sacred bond with their celestial ancestors and preserving the harmony between the physical and spiritual worlds. This connection serves as a guiding force for the Dogon, a constant reminder that they are part of a larger cosmic order that began with the birth of the Nommo, whose wisdom and presence remain interwoven with the fabric of life itself.

Chapter 4: Sirius and the Cosmic Connection

In Dogon mythology, the Sirius star system holds a revered and mystical place, representing a cosmic connection that binds humanity to the heavens. The Dogon people possess ancient knowledge of Sirius, particularly the star known as Sirius B, which is remarkable because it is invisible to the naked eye and was only confirmed by modern science in the 20th century. For the Dogon, Sirius is more than just a distant celestial body; it is the home of the Nommo, divine amphibious beings sent to Earth by the supreme creator Amma to guide humanity. The Dogon believe that the Nommo originated from Sirius and descended to Earth carrying profound knowledge, wisdom, and spiritual practices, bridging the earthly and cosmic realms in a way that suggests an intimate relationship between the stars and human life. This connection to Sirius reflects the Dogon understanding of the universe as an interconnected whole, where the heavens and Earth are bound by a shared destiny and purpose.

The Dogon people describe Sirius B as a dense, small, and incredibly heavy star that orbits the larger, brighter Sirius A. This description aligns with modern astronomical observations, which identify Sirius B as a white dwarf star—one of the densest forms of stellar remnants. According to the Dogon, Sirius B has a powerful gravitational pull and completes its orbit around Sirius A in fifty years. This information, which predates telescopic confirmation, reveals the depth of Dogon astronomical knowledge and the sophistication of their oral traditions. The Dogon attribute their knowledge of Sirius B to the teachings of the Nommo, who imparted this cosmic wisdom as part of their mission to guide humanity toward spiritual enlightenment. The Nommo's knowledge of the Sirius system illustrates a connection between humanity and the stars, suggesting that the cosmos is not merely a distant realm but a vital part of human understanding and spirituality.

In Dogon cosmology, Sirius represents more than an astronomical body; it is a source of life, energy, and spiritual guidance. The Dogon people believe that the Nommo came from Sirius to bring order to a world that was initially chaotic and incomplete. The Nommo's descent to Earth, carrying the wisdom of Sirius, marked the beginning of a harmonious relationship between humanity and the cosmos. Through rituals, teachings, and ceremonies, the Dogon maintain this connection, honoring Sirius as the origin of divine knowledge and as a guiding light that helps them align their lives with cosmic principles. This perspective on Sirius reflects a worldview in which stars are more than physical objects; they are living, spiritual entities that influence human existence and the natural order.

The significance of Sirius in Dogon spirituality is particularly evident in the Sigui ceremony, a complex, multi-year ritual held every sixty years to honor the connection between Earth and the Sirius star system. The Sigui is a sacred time of renewal, during which the Dogon reenact the creation myth, celebrate the cosmic relationship between the Nommo and humanity, and seek to realign themselves with the cycles of the universe. This ceremony reflects the Dogon belief that time is cyclical, mirroring the movements of celestial bodies and the rhythms of life. Through the Sigui, the Dogon reaffirm their bond with Sirius and the Nommo, strengthening their connection to the cosmic forces that shape their world and their destinies.

In Dogon mythology, Sirius is also viewed as a place of return, a cosmic destination that awaits souls after their earthly journey is complete. This belief in Sirius as a spiritual realm suggests that life is a continuous cycle, with the soul traveling from the stars to Earth and back to the stars. The Dogon people understand that their origins and ultimate fate are bound to Sirius, and this belief imbues their lives with a sense of purpose, as they view existence as part of a larger cosmic narrative. This idea that human life is linked to the stars underscores the Dogon worldview, where the physical and spiritual realms are not separate but intimately connected.

The Dogon's relationship with Sirius has also inspired a profound respect for knowledge and the mysteries of the universe. Through the teachings of the Nommo, the Dogon were given insight into the structure of the cosmos, learning that understanding the stars can lead to greater wisdom and spiritual growth. This knowledge encourages the Dogon to pursue harmony in all aspects of life, as they see themselves as part of a cosmic balance that must be maintained. Their understanding of Sirius reinforces the idea that knowledge is sacred, a gift that connects them to the divine and guides them on their path. This reverence for cosmic wisdom is evident in the Dogon's rituals, storytelling, and daily life, all of which are infused with a deep awareness of their connection to Sirius and the universe as a whole.

The Dogon people's view of Sirius and its connection to human life reflects a belief in the universe as an intricate web of relationships, where each star, planet, and being has a role within a greater cosmic design. For the Dogon, Sirius serves as a reminder of the unity between humanity and the cosmos, a bond that is both spiritual and physical. Through their myths, ceremonies, and ancestral teachings, the Dogon honor Sirius as the home of their divine ancestors, a source of knowledge, and a beacon that illuminates their spiritual journey. In the Dogon worldview, Sirius is not just a distant point in the night sky; it is a reminder of their origin, their purpose, and their place within the vastness of creation. Their connection to Sirius endures as a central aspect of their spirituality, guiding them to live in harmony with the universe and to seek wisdom that transcends the boundaries of the earthly realm.

Chapter 5: The Sacred Role of Twins

In Dogon mythology, twins hold a sacred and unique role, embodying profound cosmic principles of balance, duality, and harmony. The Dogon people view twins as manifestations of both the physical and spiritual realms, beings who inherently possess a connection to the dual forces that govern the universe. Twins represent the harmonious coexistence of opposites, a concept that lies at the heart of Dogon cosmology and is essential to maintaining cosmic order. The Dogon believe that Amma, the supreme creator, designed the universe with a perfect balance of male and female, light and dark, life and death. This divine equilibrium is reflected in the birth of twins, who symbolize completeness and unity, bringing with them blessings and a powerful spiritual energy that affects their family and community.

In the Dogon creation story, the Nommo, the first beings created by Amma, are themselves depicted as twins or twin-like pairs. These original Nommo were born as dual beings, representing both masculine and feminine aspects, and are often portrayed as amphibious, embodying the adaptability and fluid nature required to navigate both land and water. The Nommo's dual nature reflects Amma's vision of balance, as they serve as symbols of both physical life and spiritual wisdom. For the Dogon, the Nommo are cosmic ancestors who imparted knowledge of the universe to humanity, and their twin nature is a reminder of the divine symmetry that underpins all creation. The Dogon believe that twins born in human families carry this ancestral energy, linking them to the Nommo and the spiritual wisdom that they represent.

Twins, therefore, are seen as blessed beings, embodying the duality inherent in nature. They hold a special status within Dogon society, regarded with reverence and respect. When twins are born, their family views this event as a profound blessing and an indication of divine favor. The arrival of twins is seen as a sign that Amma's balance is manifesting within the family, providing a direct link to the cosmic principles of harmony. Their presence brings a unique energy that is believed to strengthen the family's spiritual connection to the ancestors and the cosmos. In some cases, twins are thought to possess insights or abilities that are unique to their dual nature, allowing them to act as intermediaries between the human and spiritual worlds. Their connection to each other is seen as mystical, a bond that transcends the ordinary relationships found among siblings, reflecting the spiritual and emotional unity that the Dogon believe should exist in all relationships.

To honor the sacred role of twins, the Dogon perform special rituals and ceremonies, celebrating their arrival and recognizing the dual forces they embody. These rituals are conducted not only to welcome the twins but to acknowledge and reinforce the family's commitment to harmony and respect for the divine order. The birth of twins requires careful attention and ritual, as the Dogon seek to maintain a balanced relationship with the forces that govern life and death. Families with twins often offer prayers and sacrifices to Amma and the Nommo, expressing gratitude for the blessing of twins and asking for guidance in raising them in accordance with spiritual principles. Through these rituals, the Dogon reaffirm their commitment to Amma's vision of balance, and they view the twins as both a responsibility and a privilege, bestowed upon them by the divine.

The special status of twins within Dogon culture is not only a reflection of their cosmology but also an expression of the value they place on unity and community. Twins embody the idea that strength and resilience come from working together, from maintaining a balanced relationship that honors each person's unique qualities. In this way, the Dogon see twins as role models, representing the harmonious coexistence that Amma envisioned for all beings. Their relationship is seen as an ideal, a reminder that all individuals are interconnected and that every life is part of a larger, balanced whole. The sacred role of twins reinforces the belief that duality is not about opposition but about complementarity, where each aspect supports and enhances the other, creating a unified whole. Twins also hold a place in Dogon spiritual practices, often participating in rituals and ceremonies as embodiments of the balance between life and death, the visible and invisible realms. Their presence in these rituals is believed to strengthen the connection between the human and spiritual worlds, serving as a reminder of the principles that Amma instilled in creation. In some rituals, twins are called upon to offer blessings or to lead prayers, as their unique connection to the cosmic balance is seen as a powerful force that can enhance the ritual's efficacy. Their role in these ceremonies reinforces the Dogon understanding of twins as beings who carry both ancestral wisdom and a direct link to the divine order, helping to maintain harmony within the community.

The Dogon revere twins as sacred figures who embody cosmic truths, and this reverence extends beyond their lives to their legacy within the community. Twins are believed to bring prosperity, health, and spiritual insight to their families, and their influence is thought to benefit not only their immediate relatives but the community as a whole. By honoring twins and the sacred role they play, the Dogon people reaffirm their connection to Amma and the cosmic order. They believe that, through twins, the spiritual and physical realms come closer together, making it possible for the community to live in harmony with the universe's divine principles. The birth of twins is thus a sacred event that strengthens the Dogon's commitment to the values of balance, unity, and reverence for the divine, ensuring that these principles continue to guide their lives and their society.

Chapter 6: The Symbols of Earth and Sky

In Dogon mythology, the symbols of Earth and Sky hold profound significance, representing the fundamental relationship between the physical and spiritual worlds. For the Dogon people, Earth and Sky are not merely geographical or atmospheric entities; they are powerful, living forces that embody the duality at the core of existence. This duality, often expressed in terms of male and female, order and chaos, life and death, reflects the Dogon understanding of the universe as an interconnected whole, where balance and harmony between opposing forces are essential. Earth and Sky are viewed as cosmic partners in creation, each with distinct yet complementary roles that sustain life and connect humanity to the divine. Together, they symbolize the constant interplay between the material and spiritual realms, a dynamic interaction that shapes both the Dogon worldview and their everyday lives.

In Dogon cosmology, the Earth is personified as a nurturing, feminine force known for its ability to sustain, grow, and transform. Earth is seen as the mother of all living things, a womb from which all life originates and to which all life ultimately returns. This maternal symbolism is reflected in Dogon agricultural practices, as farming is not only a means of survival but a sacred act that reconnects people with the Earth's fertility and generosity. Each planting season is approached with rituals and offerings to honor the Earth, acknowledging her role as a giver of life. Farmers consider the soil to be sacred, infused with ashe, the life force that animates all beings and objects. In Dogon society, working the land is therefore an act of respect and communion with the Earth's spirit, an acknowledgment of the deep bond between humans and the natural world. The Earth is a sacred foundation, embodying stability, endurance, and the cyclical rhythms of life, qualities that the Dogon seek to emulate in their own lives.

Sky, on the other hand, is associated with the masculine, the mysterious, and the intangible aspects of existence. The Sky represents the spiritual and celestial realms, a vast expanse that holds the stars, planets, and divine forces that influence life on Earth. In Dogon belief, the Sky is not distant or separate from humanity; rather, it is a living entity that watches over the Earth and connects the Dogon to the cosmos. The Sky is the realm of Amma, the supreme creator, and the origin of the Nommo, the divine beings who descended to Earth to guide humanity. The Dogon people believe that the movements of celestial bodies and the patterns of stars hold messages from the gods, messages that reveal truths about life, fate, and the divine order. By studying the Sky and interpreting its symbols, the Dogon gain insight into their place in the universe and the cyclical nature of time.

The relationship between Earth and Sky is symbolized by the interplay between rain and soil, elements that embody the life-giving union of masculine and feminine forces. Rain, a gift from the Sky, is seen as a divine blessing that fertilizes the Earth, allowing plants to grow and sustaining all forms of life. In Dogon rituals, rain is celebrated as a symbol of renewal and abundance, a reminder of the interdependence between the heavens and the land. The Earth, with its capacity to receive and nurture the rain, symbolizes receptivity, patience, and transformation. This union between rain and soil is central to the Dogon understanding of fertility and creation, a process that requires both active and passive forces working in harmony. Through this symbolic relationship, the Dogon people are reminded of the importance of balance, respect, and cooperation, values that extend to their relationships with each other and with the natural world.

The symbolism of Earth and Sky extends to the Dogon concept of ancestors, who are believed to dwell in both realms, bridging the material and spiritual worlds. Ancestors are thought to reside in the Sky, watching over their descendants, while their spirits remain connected to the Earth through rituals and memorials. This dual presence of ancestors reinforces the idea that Earth and Sky are not separate; they are linked by the cycle of life, death, and rebirth. By honoring the ancestors, the Dogon reaffirm their connection to both Earth and Sky, acknowledging the guidance they receive from the spiritual world while remaining rooted in the physical. The presence of ancestors in both realms strengthens the Dogon's commitment to living in harmony with the world around them, as they view life as an ongoing relationship between the living and the departed, the seen and the unseen.

Symbols of Earth and Sky are also reflected in Dogon architecture, where the design of homes, granaries, and communal spaces aligns with cosmological principles. The layout of a Dogon village often mirrors the structure of the cosmos, with the Earth represented by the central courtyard, the communal heart of life, and the Sky embodied by the surrounding structures and open spaces. Buildings are constructed using clay from the Earth, a reminder of humanity's connection to the land, while the rooftops open toward the Sky, symbolizing openness to divine guidance and cosmic wisdom. The village thus becomes a sacred space, a microcosm of the universe where Earth and Sky coexist, and where humans can feel the presence of both.

In Dogon ceremonies, masks and costumes often represent symbols of Earth and Sky, depicting animals, plants, and celestial bodies. These symbols convey messages of harmony, transformation, and the interconnectedness of life. When dancers perform rituals wearing these masks, they embody the principles of Earth and Sky, expressing the values of respect, unity, and cosmic awareness that are central to Dogon life. Through these symbols and rituals, the Dogon people cultivate a worldview that honors both the visible and invisible forces that shape their existence. Earth and Sky, with their respective qualities and energies, serve as reminders of the balance that sustains the world, a balance the Dogon strive to uphold in every aspect of their lives.

Chapter 7: Spirits of the Ancestors

In Dogon mythology, the spirits of the ancestors hold a place of reverence and respect, serving as essential connections between the living and the divine, the earthly and the celestial realms. The Dogon believe that ancestors do not simply vanish after death; instead, they transition into a spiritual form, retaining a significant role in the lives of their descendants. The spirits of the ancestors are both protectors and guides, watching over the family and the community, intervening in times of need, and offering wisdom to those who seek their counsel. For the Dogon, honoring these spirits is a way of staying connected to the past, acknowledging the sacrifices and legacies of those who came before, and ensuring the continuity of cultural traditions and values. Ancestor veneration is therefore a fundamental aspect of Dogon spiritual life, reinforcing the bond between the living and the spiritual world.

The transition from life to the ancestral realm is seen as a journey, one in which the deceased moves through stages to become a full spirit. The Dogon believe that the soul must be guided to the ancestral world, a process that requires proper rituals and ceremonies. These rituals are performed by the family and community to ensure that the spirit reaches its destination and becomes a benevolent force that can watch over the family. One of the most important ceremonies for this purpose is the *dama*, a complex and elaborate ritual that helps the spirit of the deceased move to the world of the ancestors. During the dama, the Dogon people engage in dancing, drumming, and the wearing of sacred masks that represent both the spirit of the deceased and the forces that govern the natural and supernatural realms. The dama ceremony not only honors the individual but also renews the bond between the living community and the spiritual world, reinforcing the sense of continuity and interdependence.

The Dogon believe that once the deceased successfully enters the ancestral realm, they join a community of spirits who maintain a strong connection with the living world. These ancestral spirits are regarded as a part of the family and community, as they continue to watch over their descendants, offering guidance, protection, and wisdom. The spirits are thought to have special insights into both the human and spiritual worlds, as they exist in a state that transcends physical limitations. They are consulted through rituals and offerings, especially in times of crisis or important life decisions, as their wisdom and perspective are believed to provide clarity and direction. Ancestral spirits are not distant or removed from daily life; they are considered active participants in family matters, influencing everything from health and prosperity to harmony within relationships.

To honor the spirits of the ancestors, the Dogon people practice rituals that often involve offerings, prayers, and acts of remembrance. These offerings, which can include food, drink, and small symbolic objects, are made at shrines dedicated to the ancestors. These shrines are sacred spaces, believed to serve as portals through which the spirits of the ancestors can be present in the physical world. When making offerings, the Dogon communicate directly with their ancestors, expressing gratitude, seeking protection, or asking for advice. Through these acts, they reaffirm their connection to those who have passed and acknowledge the ongoing influence of ancestral spirits in their lives. This continuous relationship with the ancestors reinforces the Dogon view that life is a cycle, one that involves birth, death, and rebirth, with each stage interwoven into the community's spiritual fabric.

Ancestral spirits are especially important in guiding younger generations, as they embody the values, knowledge, and cultural traditions that the Dogon hold sacred. By honoring their ancestors, the Dogon pass down a legacy that transcends individual lifetimes, emphasizing continuity and cultural preservation. The spirits of the ancestors are seen as custodians of tradition, and through their influence, they ensure that each generation remains aligned with the values that have defined Dogon identity for centuries. This connection is particularly reinforced during initiation ceremonies, where young people are introduced to the sacred teachings of the ancestors, learning about the responsibilities they bear toward family, community, and the natural world. These teachings emphasize respect, communal support, and the importance of living in harmony with the universe, values that are at the heart of Dogon culture and spirituality.

In Dogon art and ritual, the spirits of the ancestors are symbolized through masks, sculptures, and images that capture their presence and power. The Dogon people create masks that represent the spirits during ceremonies, each mask embodying the characteristics of specific ancestors or elements of the natural world associated with them. These masks are not mere decorations; they are sacred objects believed to channel the energy of the spirits, allowing the Dogon to communicate with the ancestors directly during rituals. When these masks are worn in ceremonies, it is as if the spirits themselves are present, guiding the community and bestowing blessings. Through dance, music, and ritual movements, the Dogon bring the spirits of the ancestors into the midst of their gatherings, creating an environment where the past and present merge, and where the wisdom of the ancestors can flow freely among the living.

The role of ancestral spirits extends beyond guidance and protection to include the enforcement of moral and ethical standards within the community. The Dogon believe that the ancestors observe the actions of the living and that they have the power to bless or punish, depending on whether the community is upholding its values. By living in accordance with the principles taught by the ancestors, the Dogon people seek to earn their blessings, ensuring peace, prosperity, and harmony.

This spiritual accountability reinforces social cohesion, as each member of the community understands their responsibility to honor the legacy of those who came before them. For the Dogon, the spirits of the ancestors are not only protectors but also moral guides, ensuring that each generation carries forward the traditions, wisdom, and strength of the Dogon heritage. Through their enduring influence, the spirits of the ancestors create a living legacy, a constant reminder of the unbroken bond between past and present, the visible and the unseen, and the unity that defines Dogon existence.

Chapter 8: Rituals of Fertility and Harvest

In Dogon culture, the rituals of fertility and harvest are sacred ceremonies that celebrate the life-giving forces of nature and the interconnectedness of all things. These rituals are performed to honor the Earth's bounty, acknowledge the spiritual powers that govern growth and abundance, and ensure the continued prosperity of the community. For the Dogon, fertility and harvest are not solely agricultural processes; they are deeply spiritual events that require the harmonious cooperation of the physical and spiritual realms. The rituals of fertility and harvest represent a reciprocal relationship between the people and the Earth, a partnership that emphasizes respect, gratitude, and responsibility toward the land and its resources. Through these ceremonies, the Dogon reaffirm their commitment to living in balance with the natural world, a world they view as infused with the presence of divine forces and ancestral spirits.

The cycle of fertility and harvest begins with rituals dedicated to Osanyin, the Orisha of herbs, plants, and natural healing powers. These rituals acknowledge the role of Osanyin and other nature spirits in nurturing and protecting crops, as well as providing the Dogon people with sustenance and medicinal resources. Farmers call upon Osanyin's blessing for fertile soil, abundant rains, and protection against pests and drought, knowing that these natural elements are essential for a successful harvest. During these ceremonies, offerings of water, seeds, and symbolic items are made, representing the community's gratitude for the gifts of the land. These offerings are placed at specific shrines or sacred spaces within the fields, marking these areas as hallowed ground where the divine meets the Earth.

One of the most important fertility rituals in Dogon culture is performed during the planting season, a time when the community comes together to invoke blessings for a bountiful yield. The Dogon believe that fertility is not solely about the productivity of the land but also about the generative forces of life that govern both people and nature. The ritual often involves a procession to the fields, where prayers and songs are offered to the Earth, requesting her to nurture the seeds and transform them into plentiful crops. Women play a significant role in these fertility rituals, symbolizing their connection to creation and the nurturing aspects of life. Their participation is seen as essential for invoking the Earth's reproductive power, as they embody the principles of growth, care, and continuity that sustain the community. Through their songs and dances, the women channel energies that are believed to activate the fertility of the land, infusing it with the life force needed to bring forth abundance.

As the growing season progresses, the Dogon community continues to honor the spirits of the Earth and sky through small rituals and daily acts of reverence. Each phase of growth is marked by gratitude and mindfulness, as farmers observe the transformation of seeds into crops, a process they understand as a sacred unfolding of the Earth's gifts. The Dogon view each plant as a manifestation of divine energy, a testament to the Earth's ability to sustain and renew life. This perspective inspires a deep respect for the land, as the community recognizes the dependence of human life on the health and well-being of the natural world. By maintaining a close relationship with the land, the Dogon ensure that their practices remain sustainable, and they treat each harvest as a sacred exchange rather than merely an extraction of resources.

At the end of the growing season, the Dogon people prepare for the harvest, a time of great celebration and reverence. The harvest rituals are elaborate and joyful, symbolizing both the fulfillment of the Earth's promise and the gratitude of the community for the abundance they have received. These ceremonies often involve communal feasting, singing, and dancing, all performed in honor of the spirits that govern fertility and growth. The first harvested crops are dedicated to the ancestors and deities, a gesture that acknowledges the sacred relationship between the people, the land, and the divine. By offering the first fruits of the harvest, the Dogon demonstrate their respect and gratitude, ensuring that the spirits are honored and that the balance between the material and spiritual realms is maintained.

During the harvest festival, the Dogon people also perform rituals that renew and strengthen communal bonds, recognizing that fertility and abundance are not just individual gains but blessings meant to be shared by all. Elders and community leaders lead these ceremonies, reinforcing the values of unity, cooperation, and collective responsibility. These rituals are a reminder that the prosperity of the land is tied to the well-being of the entire community and that each person has a role to play in maintaining harmony with the Earth. By sharing the harvest, the Dogon ensure that no one is left out, and they celebrate the communal spirit that has helped them endure through generations.

An important aspect of the harvest rituals is the honoring of ancestral spirits, who are believed to protect and guide the people throughout the agricultural cycle. The Dogon attribute their success to the blessings of these spirits, who have passed down the knowledge and wisdom needed to cultivate the land and sustain life. By invoking the ancestors during the harvest, the Dogon acknowledge their debt to the past and affirm their commitment to preserving this legacy for future generations. The spirits of the ancestors are considered guardians of the community's prosperity, and their presence in the rituals symbolizes the unbroken connection between the past, present, and future. This ancestral bond reinforces the Dogon's sense of identity and continuity, grounding them in a tradition that has both spiritual and practical importance.

Through the rituals of fertility and harvest, the Dogon people maintain a living connection to the land, their ancestors, and the divine. These ceremonies reflect a deep understanding of life's cycles, emphasizing the need for balance, respect, and gratitude. By honoring the Earth's fertility and celebrating the harvest, the Dogon ensure the preservation of their culture, their environment, and their relationship with the sacred forces that sustain them. Each planting, growing, and harvest season becomes a renewal of faith, a reminder of the community's interdependence with nature, and a testament to the enduring power of their spiritual heritage.

Chapter 9: Masks, Dances, and Divine Communication

In Dogon culture, masks and dances hold an essential place as forms of divine communication, providing a means to connect with spiritual forces and honor the ancestors. These ceremonies are more than mere performances; they are sacred rituals that allow the Dogon people to bridge the gap between the physical world and the realms of the divine. Each mask and movement carries deep symbolic meaning, representing various aspects of the Dogon cosmology, spiritual beliefs, and respect for the unseen forces that influence daily life. Through these practices, the Dogon express their reverence for the natural and supernatural, finding ways to celebrate, invoke, and appease the spirits that guide and protect their communities. The role of masks and dances goes beyond artistry; it is rooted in a rich tradition of ritual and spirituality, embodying the Dogon's connection to their ancestors, the Earth, and the cosmos.

Masks are considered sacred objects, each one crafted with meticulous care and imbued with spiritual power. These masks are not mere decorations; they are seen as living symbols, designed to convey the presence of spirits, deities, and ancestral forces. Each mask has its own character and story, representing different elements of Dogon mythology, including the spirits of animals, nature, and ancestors. Some masks are dedicated to the Nommo, the primordial beings created by Amma, the supreme god, while others represent the forces of nature, such as the earth, wind, and water. The process of creating a mask is an act of devotion and involves rituals that prepare the mask to serve as a vessel for divine energy. Mask-makers, often esteemed members of the community, are responsible for imbuing each piece with its intended spirit, a task that requires knowledge of spiritual symbols and a deep understanding of Dogon cosmology.

During ceremonies, these masks are worn by dancers who bring them to life, transforming themselves into the spirits they represent. The dancers are believed to channel the spirits through their movements, embodying their characteristics and powers. This act of transformation is sacred, and it requires ritual preparation, including prayers, offerings, and sometimes fasting, to ensure that the dancer is spiritually prepared to carry the weight of the mask's divine energy. When the dancers don their masks, they enter a state that allows them to communicate with the unseen, acting as intermediaries between the physical and spiritual realms. The masks thus become more than objects; they are transformed into divine beings, allowing the Dogon to interact with their ancestors and the cosmic forces that shape their world.

The dances performed with these masks are filled with symbolic gestures and movements, each step and motion carrying meaning that is understood by the community. Some dances mimic the movements of animals, celebrating the connection between the Dogon and the natural world, while others represent cosmic events or cycles, reflecting the Dogon understanding of the universe and the role of humanity within it. The dances can vary from slow, deliberate movements that signify contemplation and reverence to fast, powerful motions that evoke strength, vitality, and the intensity of the spiritual forces being honored. Each dance is a form of storytelling, revealing narratives that teach, inspire, and remind the Dogon of their shared heritage, values, and connection to the divine.

The masks and dances are particularly important during ceremonies such as the *dama*, a ritual held to honor the spirits of the deceased and guide them to the ancestral realm. During the dama, the dancers wear masks representing various ancestors and spirits, enacting movements that signify the journey from life to the afterlife. This ceremony helps the community come to terms with loss, celebrate the lives of those who have passed, and ensure that the souls of the deceased are peacefully integrated into the spirit world. Through the dances and masks, the Dogon believe they can communicate directly with their ancestors, expressing gratitude, asking for guidance, and seeking blessings. The *dama* is not only a time of mourning but also one of renewal, as it strengthens the bond between the living and the dead, reaffirming the continuity of life that transcends the boundaries of mortality.

Masks and dances are also integral to rituals that seek to bring harmony and balance to the community, especially during times of conflict or hardship. The Dogon believe that performing these sacred rituals can help restore equilibrium by invoking the spirits and ancestors to intervene on their behalf. For instance, during times of drought or famine, masks representing rain spirits are worn in dances that call for the return of rainfall, embodying the community's desire for relief and abundance. These dances are not merely symbolic; they are believed to be powerful acts that attract the attention of spiritual forces, encouraging them to respond to the needs of the people. Through this interaction with the divine, the Dogon reaffirm their reliance on the unseen world and the forces that govern the natural cycles of life and sustenance.

The masks and dances also serve as a means of education for the younger generation, teaching them about the myths, values, and cosmology of the Dogon people. Children and young adults are encouraged to observe and participate in these rituals, gradually learning the significance of each mask, each movement, and each gesture. Through this process, they come to understand the complexities of their culture and the importance of maintaining a respectful relationship with the spiritual realm. The knowledge and skills associated with creating masks, performing dances, and interpreting their meanings are passed down from generation to generation, preserving the Dogon heritage and ensuring that the wisdom of the ancestors endures.

In Dogon society, the masks and dances are more than just cultural expressions; they are profound spiritual practices that connect the community to the divine and to each other. By embodying the spirits, the dancers create a sacred space where the boundaries between human and divine blur, allowing the Dogon to experience the presence of their ancestors and the cosmic forces that shape their lives. Through the ritual use of masks and dances, the Dogon reinforce their worldview, one in which all life is interwoven with the spiritual, and where communication with the unseen is an essential part of maintaining harmony, balance, and a sense of belonging within the cosmos.

Chapter 10: The Dogon Mysteries and Modern Fascination

The Dogon people have long captivated the imagination of scholars, researchers, and spiritual seekers due to their rich mythology, complex cosmology, and profound understanding of the natural and celestial worlds. Among the Dogon mysteries that have fascinated modern audiences is their intricate knowledge of the Sirius star system, especially their apparent awareness of Sirius B, a dense white dwarf star that orbits Sirius A. This specific astronomical knowledge, believed to have been part of Dogon tradition long before modern telescopes confirmed the existence of Sirius B, has raised questions about the origins of Dogon cosmology and the sources of their wisdom. The Dogon assert that this knowledge came from the Nommo, amphibious, divine beings whom they believe descended from Sirius and imparted the Dogon with sacred teachings on the universe, the cycles of life, and the laws of harmony. The idea that such precise astronomical information could be embedded in an oral tradition has generated widespread curiosity and led to speculation about the possible sources of Dogon knowledge.

The modern fascination with the Dogon began in earnest when French anthropologists Marcel Griaule and Germaine Dieterlen published their findings in the mid-20th century after spending decades studying Dogon culture. They documented the Dogon's knowledge of Sirius B and their belief in its fifty-year orbit, sparking discussions that reached beyond anthropology and into fields like astronomy, archaeology, and even theories of extraterrestrial influence. Some writers and researchers have suggested that the Dogon's knowledge of Sirius B could not have come solely from observational methods available to an isolated community in Mali, especially given the star's invisibility to the naked eye. This speculation has inspired hypotheses that the Dogon may have had contact with ancient visitors from other worlds, or that their ancestors were custodians of a lost, advanced civilization whose understanding of astronomy far exceeded what was known in other ancient cultures.

While such theories captivate popular imagination, scholars caution against dismissing the complexity of oral traditions and indigenous knowledge systems. The Dogon's cosmology is deeply symbolic, blending mythology with observations of the natural world in ways that may appear enigmatic to outsiders but are highly coherent within Dogon cultural and spiritual frameworks. For the Dogon, knowledge is not only empirical but also spiritual, derived from their reverence for the Nommo and their belief that these divine ancestors conveyed essential truths about the universe. The Dogon view the cosmos as an interconnected web of relationships, in which every being, planet, and star has a role in maintaining balance. The Sirius star system, with its cycles and motions, reflects this balance and serves as a celestial guide for understanding life's deeper mysteries. Modern fascination with Dogon cosmology, however, often overlooks the cultural context in which this knowledge is embedded, seeking to explain it solely through scientific or speculative frameworks rather than appreciating it as a spiritual and symbolic system.

The Dogon's unique approach to cosmology has influenced various modern thinkers who find in their worldview a refreshing alternative to purely materialistic or reductionist interpretations of the universe. Writers, artists, and spiritual leaders are drawn to the Dogon's holistic understanding of existence, which integrates the physical and metaphysical realms. The Dogon belief in ashe, the life force that flows through all things, resonates with people seeking a sense of interconnectedness and purpose. This interest has led to a renewed appreciation for indigenous cosmologies and their capacity to offer insights into humanity's relationship with the universe. For many, the Dogon's teachings on balance, duality, and the sacred relationship between Earth and sky inspire reflection on how modern society approaches science, nature, and spirituality. In addition to their cosmology, the Dogon's rich mythology, rituals, and symbols also continue to captivate modern audiences. Elements like their elaborate mask dances, which serve as a bridge between the physical and spiritual realms, have influenced Western art and performance. The Dogon use masks and dances as a means of divine communication, invoking the spirits of ancestors, deities, and nature to celebrate life, honor death, and reinforce community bonds. These performances embody principles of balance, harmony, and respect for the unseen, reminding audiences of the sacredness of life's cycles. For the Dogon, each mask and movement represents a connection to the divine, and their dances are profound expressions of their spiritual beliefs. Modern audiences, in turn, view these practices with awe, appreciating the sophistication and spiritual depth of a people who use ritual as a means to engage with the mysteries of existence.

However, this fascination with the Dogon has also led to misunderstandings and, in some cases, exoticization. Often, outsiders approach Dogon knowledge as an isolated mystery rather than understanding it as part of a broader African tradition of cosmological thought. The Dogon are sometimes cast as keepers of a "lost" knowledge, rather than as a community whose understanding of the world has grown through centuries of observation, introspection, and ritual. As a result, some interpretations of Dogon mythology have tended to overshadow the fact that the Dogon's insights are deeply rooted in their cultural and environmental context, developed over generations of interaction with the natural world and guided by a philosophy that values both material knowledge and spiritual wisdom.

The modern fascination with the Dogon and their mysteries reflects humanity's enduring search for answers to life's most profound questions. As people from different cultures look to the Dogon for insight, they are reminded that there are diverse ways of understanding existence and that ancient wisdom has much to offer in an age often dominated by technological perspectives. The Dogon's spiritual connection to the stars, their reverence for ancestors, and their commitment to maintaining balance between humanity and nature stand as timeless principles that continue to inspire those who seek a deeper understanding of their place in the cosmos. This cross-cultural interest underscores the universal appeal of the Dogon's cosmology and mythology, highlighting how ancient beliefs can resonate across time and space, offering valuable insights into the nature of life, purpose, and the mysteries that bind humanity to the universe.

BOOK 3
ZULU MYTHOLOGY
THUNDERS OF THE SKY: THE MYTHS AND LEGENDS OF ZULU GODS
SAMUEL SHEPHERD

Chapter 1: In the Beginning of Time

In Zulu mythology, the story of creation unfolds with a sense of reverence and wonder for the mysteries of existence. At the beginning of time, there was only Umvelinqangi, the Great Spirit and Creator, who existed in silence and vastness before the world came into being. Umvelinqangi is both powerful and enigmatic, embodying the primal forces that would eventually shape all of life. His name, meaning "He Who Was in the Very Beginning," captures his role as the source of creation, the being who contains within himself all potential and life. The Zulu people believe that from this eternal, formless existence, Umvelinqangi brought forth the fundamental elements that would give rise to the Earth, the sky, and the beings that would inhabit them.

The act of creation began when Umvelinqangi sent forth a great wind, a breath that moved through the void, marking the beginning of movement and transformation. This wind, known as Moya, symbolizes the breath of life and is believed to carry the essence of Umvelinqangi, connecting all living things to the Creator. Moya swept through the vast emptiness, stirring it into motion and preparing it for the arrival of life. In Zulu belief, Moya is more than just a wind; it is the life force that flows through all creation, a reminder that every being is touched by the divine breath of Umvelinqangi and connected to the same sacred source. This wind signaled the transition from formlessness to form, from silence to sound, setting the stage for the unfolding of the physical world.

Umvelinqangi's next act was to create uHlanga, the great reed, which emerged from the earth, reaching toward the heavens. The uHlanga represents the origin of all life, a sacred plant that embodies the connection between the earthly and the spiritual realms. It is from this reed that life emerged, according to Zulu tradition, with the first ancestors and the creatures of the world being born from its shoots. The uHlanga is a symbol of birth, growth, and unity, as it connects the earth to the sky, representing the flow of life that runs from one generation to the next. For the Zulu, the uHlanga is not merely a plant but a sacred reminder of the oneness of all life, as every person, animal, and plant is believed to share the same divine origin.

The first beings to emerge from uHlanga were Unkulunkulu, the Great Ancestor, and the other original ancestors who would populate the Earth and begin the lineage of the Zulu people. Unkulunkulu, whose name means "The Great-Great One," is seen as the progenitor of humanity, the one who set the world in motion by bringing people, animals, and plants into existence. Emerging from the reed, Unkulunkulu grew to full strength and became the first to understand the natural laws of the Earth, learning the ways of fire, water, and the cycles of life. He is credited with teaching humanity the skills necessary for survival, including hunting, gathering, and the art of building shelters. As the first human, Unkulunkulu serves as both a father and a guide to the Zulu, embodying the wisdom and strength needed to live in harmony with the land and with each other.

Unkulunkulu's creation of humanity and his role as the first ancestor highlight the Zulu emphasis on community and interconnectedness. In Zulu cosmology, individuals are seen not as separate entities but as integral parts of a larger collective that includes their ancestors, the natural world, and the spirit of Umvelinqangi. This belief fosters a deep sense of responsibility and respect for the community, as each generation understands itself as a continuation of the life that began with Unkulunkulu and Umvelinqangi. To honor their ancestors, the Zulu people engage in rituals and ceremonies that strengthen the bond between the living and those who came before them, paying homage to the continuity of life that began in the beginning of time.

Chapter 2: Amma, the Supreme Creator

In Dogon mythology, Amma is the supreme creator, the source from which all existence flows, and the central force behind the creation and order of the universe. Amma is portrayed as a being of immense power and knowledge, embodying both male and female aspects, which represent the unity and duality that define all life and creation. Amma existed alone in the vast, silent void before time and matter took form. Within this formless expanse, Amma contained all possibilities, holding within divine essence the potential for light and darkness, life and death, order and chaos. From this state of unity, Amma began the process of creation, an act that would forever transform the void into a vibrant cosmos filled with celestial bodies, spiritual beings, and earthly life.

One of the first acts of Amma's creation was the formation of a cosmic egg, a powerful and sacred structure that held within it the seeds of the universe. This cosmic egg represented the entirety of existence in its latent form, a microcosm that contained the essential elements of life, light, and the future forms of stars, planets, and even the souls of living beings. For the Dogon, the cosmic egg is a powerful symbol of beginnings and potential, capturing the idea that all things are interconnected and stem from a common origin. Within the egg, Amma placed twin spirals, symbolizing the balance of male and female, light and darkness, and other essential dualities that would later define the structure of the universe. The presence of these twin spirals reflects Amma's dedication to balance and harmony, qualities that were essential to sustaining the universe and all its creations.

Amma's act of creation did not end with the cosmic egg; rather, it was the beginning of a series of actions that would continue to unfold. Inside the cosmic egg, Amma introduced elements and forces that would give rise to the Nommo, a set of divine, amphibious beings who would play an essential role in the world Amma was shaping. The Nommo were created in pairs, reflecting the same duality Amma had built into the fabric of the universe. Each pair of Nommo represented a union of opposites—male and female, strength and gentleness, action and contemplation. As beings of both water and spirit, the Nommo served as mediators between the spiritual and physical worlds. They embodied Amma's desire for unity and balance, bringing harmony to a world that was still in the process of being formed.

Amma's creation of the Nommo was significant not only for their roles as spiritual guides but also because they embodied the principles of order and knowledge. Amma imbued the Nommo with wisdom, granting them insights into the structure and laws of the universe. The Dogon believe that these beings were tasked with bringing this divine wisdom to humanity, helping people understand their place within the cosmic order and the importance of living in harmony with nature and spiritual forces. As emissaries of Amma, the Nommo were sent to Earth to teach humans sacred knowledge, including the rhythms of the cosmos, agricultural practices, and the principles of balance and community that would allow them to thrive. The Dogon people view the Nommo as the link between themselves and Amma, bridging the divine will of the creator with the lived experiences of humanity.

In addition to creating the Nommo, Amma introduced other elements into the cosmos to further define the nature of existence. One of these elements was Yurugu, or the Pale Fox, a being who, unlike the harmonious Nommo, embodied disruption and imperfection. According to Dogon mythology, Yurugu was born prematurely, separating himself from the cosmic egg before Amma's creation was complete. This act of defiance introduced imbalance and conflict into the universe, making Yurugu a symbol of chaos, disorder, and incompletion. However, Amma allowed Yurugu to exist, recognizing that the imperfections he brought were also part of the universal balance. In Dogon thought, Yurugu's existence reminds humanity that life contains both harmony and discord, and that challenges and struggles are integral to the cycle of creation and growth.

Amma's interaction with Yurugu and the Nommo demonstrates the importance of balance in Dogon cosmology. Amma did not seek to eliminate Yurugu's influence but instead incorporated it into the cosmic structure. This acceptance of both order and chaos reflects the Dogon belief in the necessity of dualities, the understanding that true harmony requires the coexistence of opposing forces. Through Amma's actions, the Dogon are taught that both perfection and imperfection are needed to create a complete, meaningful existence. The Nommo, with their wisdom and harmonious nature, guide humanity toward balance, while Yurugu reminds them that the path is not without challenges and that growth often arises from overcoming adversity.

As Amma continued to shape the universe, the dual forces of harmony and discord continued to play their roles, creating a dynamic and evolving cosmos. The Dogon view Amma's ongoing act of creation as an expression of divine patience and attention to detail, where every element, no matter how small, has a purpose within the grand design. Amma's creative actions are celebrated through rituals and ceremonies that honor the ongoing process of creation, as the Dogon believe that Amma's influence remains present in the cycles of nature and the lives of all beings. This reverence for Amma and the creation story is central to Dogon spirituality, a reminder that they are part of a vast and complex universe governed by balance, wisdom, and respect for both order and the unknown.

In Dogon culture, the story of Amma's creation is not just a myth but a framework that shapes how they understand their existence and purpose. Amma's actions and the beings brought forth through divine will serve as both a reminder of their cosmic origins and a guide for living in harmony with the world around them. Through Amma, the Dogon are connected to a timeless creation, one that teaches them about balance, resilience, and the sacredness of all life within the vast tapestry of the universe.

Chapter 3: The Birth of the Nommo

In Dogon mythology, the birth of the Nommo is a foundational event that shapes not only the structure of the universe but also the spiritual framework of human life. The Nommo, revered as the first divine beings created by Amma, the supreme creator, are central figures in Dogon cosmology. They embody duality, wisdom, and cosmic order, representing both the physical and spiritual realms. Their birth is viewed as a powerful act of creation that introduced balance into a universe that was previously void and formless. According to Dogon belief, Amma created the Nommo from the essence of water, which is symbolic of life, fluidity, and connection. This connection to water reflects the Nommo's ability to bridge worlds and sustain life, marking them as both creators and guides for humanity. As beings of duality, the Nommo are typically represented as pairs, embodying the male and female aspects that Amma wove into the fabric of existence. This duality is not only a reflection of the physical world but also serves as a reminder of the balance that governs all life.

The Dogon view the Nommo as amphibious, water-dwelling entities who possess both human and serpent-like characteristics, making them adaptable, fluid, and deeply connected to the life-giving properties of water. The Nommo's association with water is significant, as water represents the essential, nourishing force that sustains all creation. In Dogon thought, water is the element that allows for transformation, growth, and the movement between realms. The Nommo, as beings born of water, are seen as bearers of life, capable of guiding souls and influencing the cycles of nature. Their amphibious form reinforces their role as intermediaries, beings who are at once earthly and divine, able to navigate both the physical and spiritual domains with ease. This unique nature makes them the ideal messengers and teachers, sent by Amma to impart sacred knowledge to humanity and ensure that the balance within creation is maintained.

The Dogon believe that the Nommo were born within the cosmic egg, a structure that Amma created to hold the potential for all life and existence. Within this egg, the forces of duality and unity coexisted in a state of profound balance, embodying Amma's vision for the universe. The Nommo's birth from this egg was a momentous event, signifying the emergence of order, knowledge, and purpose within the cosmos. By bringing the Nommo into existence, Amma infused the universe with beings who could uphold the sacred principles of harmony and interconnectedness. Each pair of Nommo was imbued with a unique role and purpose, making them distinct yet complementary beings who contributed to the overall balance of creation. Their dual nature emphasizes the Dogon understanding of cosmic order, where opposing forces work together rather than in conflict, fostering a unity that is essential for life's sustainability.

As soon as the Nommo emerged, they began the task of organizing the universe according to Amma's will, shaping both the seen and unseen worlds. They brought forth knowledge of the stars, the cycles of the seasons, and the principles of agriculture, all of which were crucial for human survival and prosperity. The Dogon revere the Nommo as the source of their sacred teachings on the rhythms of the cosmos, viewing them as bearers of wisdom who provided guidance on how to live in harmony with the natural world. One of the most profound teachings attributed to the Nommo is the knowledge of the Sirius star system, particularly Sirius B, which the Dogon believe is the Nommo's celestial origin. The Dogon possess a detailed understanding of Sirius, including the fifty-year orbit of Sirius B around Sirius A, a fact that has both puzzled and fascinated modern researchers. The Dogon credit the Nommo with imparting this cosmic knowledge, seeing it as part of the divine wisdom that shapes their worldview and connection to the stars.

The Nommo also introduced rituals and ceremonies that would allow the Dogon people to communicate with the spiritual world and honor the cycles of life, death, and rebirth. They taught the Dogon how to perform sacred rites, the use of masks in ceremonies, and the significance of ancestor veneration. Through these practices, the Nommo established a cultural and spiritual foundation that the Dogon continue to observe, ensuring that each generation remains connected to their origins and to the divine forces that influence their lives. These rituals are not merely symbolic; they are living expressions of the Dogon's relationship with the Nommo and the cosmos, reenacting the creation story and reaffirming their place within the universe. By maintaining these rituals, the Dogon believe they honor the Nommo's legacy, keeping alive the sacred knowledge passed down from the first beings who shaped their existence.

Beyond imparting knowledge and guiding the Dogon in spiritual practices, the Nommo are seen as protectors who continue to watch over humanity and the world. Their presence is invoked in times of need, as they are believed to have the power to restore balance and heal disruptions in the natural order. When the community faces crises, whether related to health, weather, or conflict, the Dogon turn to the Nommo for protection and intervention, calling upon their wisdom to restore harmony. The Nommo's role as guardians is an extension of their original purpose, as they were born to sustain the universe and support all forms of life within it. This belief in the Nommo's protective power strengthens the Dogon's sense of connection to the divine and reinforces their understanding of life as a journey guided by forces beyond the visible.

In Dogon cosmology, the birth of the Nommo is an ongoing source of inspiration, wisdom, and spiritual guidance. They are not simply mythological figures but foundational beings who embody the principles of duality, balance, and divine knowledge. Through the Nommo, the Dogon have established a way of life that honors the interconnectedness of all things and recognizes the sacred order that Amma initiated at the beginning of time. The Nommo's teachings continue to shape Dogon society, reminding each generation of their cosmic heritage and the responsibility to live in harmony with the universe.

Chapter 4: Sirius and the Cosmic Connection

In Dogon mythology, the Sirius star system holds a profound place, representing an essential cosmic connection that binds humanity to the stars and the divine. For the Dogon people, Sirius is not simply a distant celestial body but a realm of deep spiritual significance, often referred to as the home of the Nommo, the divine beings who descended to Earth as messengers and guides. The Nommo, whom the Dogon believe to be amphibious, ancestral spirits, were sent by Amma, the supreme creator, to bring knowledge, order, and sacred teachings to humanity. This connection to Sirius underscores the Dogon worldview that the cosmos is an interconnected web of relationships and influences, where the stars, planets, and human life are all intertwined within a shared divine plan. The belief that the Nommo came from Sirius reinforces a sense of cosmic kinship, establishing a spiritual and symbolic link between the Dogon people and the vast universe beyond.

One of the most intriguing aspects of Dogon cosmology is their intricate knowledge of the Sirius star system, particularly the star Sirius B, which is invisible to the naked eye and was confirmed by modern astronomers only in the 20th century. The Dogon, however, have long held oral traditions describing Sirius B as a small, dense star that orbits Sirius A in a cycle of approximately fifty years. This knowledge has intrigued researchers and raised questions about the origins of Dogon astronomy, as the existence of Sirius B is not something that could easily be observed without modern technology. According to the Dogon, this knowledge was imparted to them by the Nommo, who carried with them cosmic wisdom from Sirius to share with humanity. For the Dogon, the connection to Sirius B is not merely a matter of scientific curiosity; it is a deeply spiritual link, a reminder that human existence is woven into a larger cosmic order and that the mysteries of the universe hold wisdom that can guide human life.

The Dogon people view Sirius and its stars as symbols of cycles, balance, and continuity, values that are central to their understanding of life and the natural world. The fifty-year orbit of Sirius B around Sirius A is mirrored in certain Dogon ceremonies, particularly the Sigui festival, which takes place every sixty years to honor the alignment of Earth with the Sirius star system. This festival is a sacred time of renewal, reflection, and cosmic reconnection. During the Sigui, the Dogon reenact their creation story, celebrate the teachings of the Nommo, and reestablish their spiritual bond with the heavens. For the Dogon, this alignment of their ceremonies with the cycles of Sirius emphasizes the importance of harmony between Earth and the cosmos, reinforcing the belief that humanity is not isolated but part of a vast, interconnected network of energies and influences.

The spiritual connection to Sirius extends beyond ceremony, shaping the Dogon's worldview and their understanding of the role of humanity within the universe. The Dogon believe that Sirius is a source of life, energy, and knowledge, a beacon that guides them toward greater understanding and awareness. Through their myths and teachings, the Dogon express the idea that humanity is influenced by celestial forces and that the alignment with Sirius serves as a reminder of the unity between the physical and spiritual realms. This relationship between Sirius and the Dogon people reflects a belief that knowledge of the stars is not merely for understanding the heavens but also for gaining insight into the human experience and the principles that govern existence. The Dogon hold that by studying the cycles and movements of Sirius, they can learn about the cycles of life, death, and rebirth, as well as the natural order that Amma established in the universe.

The teachings of the Nommo and the influence of Sirius have shaped Dogon rituals, values, and daily practices, grounding their community in a worldview that celebrates both earthly and cosmic harmony. In Dogon thought, the stars are living entities, each with its role and purpose, contributing to the balance of the universe. This belief imbues Sirius with a sacred presence, a guiding light that embodies both the mystery and the knowledge of the cosmos. By looking to Sirius, the Dogon people find inspiration to live with integrity, compassion, and respect for the cycles of nature. Sirius is viewed not only as a physical star but as a spiritual force that binds the Dogon to their ancestors, their creator, and the universe at large.

In addition to the connection with the Nommo, the Dogon see Sirius as part of a cosmic relationship that includes both the living and the deceased. Ancestral spirits are believed to be tied to Sirius, existing in a realm that parallels the physical world. The Dogon hold that these spirits can guide and protect their descendants, acting as intermediaries between the human world and the cosmos. This belief in the ancestral presence within the Sirius system reinforces the Dogon perspective that the cosmos is filled with consciousness, with every celestial body holding a purpose and a connection to humanity. By venerating Sirius and their ancestors, the Dogon keep alive the understanding that life on Earth is part of a larger cosmic journey, one that transcends the boundaries of birth and death.

The knowledge of Sirius and the teachings of the Nommo have also influenced Dogon art, symbols, and cosmological expressions, particularly in their rituals, carvings, and sacred masks. These symbols are crafted not only to honor the cosmos but to serve as conduits for cosmic energies, allowing the Dogon to embody the principles of Sirius within their spiritual practices. By creating art that reflects the structure of the Sirius star system, the Dogon bring the cosmic forces into their daily lives, reinforcing their connection to the stars and their role in the divine plan established by Amma. This integration of cosmic symbolism in their art is a testament to the Dogon's understanding of life as interconnected with the celestial, where every act, symbol, and ceremony carries a sacred resonance that aligns them with the cosmos.

The Dogon's relationship with Sirius represents a way of seeing the universe as a unified, purposeful entity, where humanity is an integral part of a grand design. This perspective provides them with a sense of belonging to something much larger than themselves, a cosmic family that includes the stars, ancestors, and divine beings like the Nommo. The belief that Sirius is both a source of wisdom and a guide for life endows the Dogon's existence with purpose, instilling in them the values of harmony, respect, and cosmic awareness. Through their connection to Sirius, the Dogon find a pathway to understanding the mysteries of life and the universe, guided by a star that links them to their origins, their ancestors, and their place within the cosmos.

Chapter 5: The Sacred Role of Twins

In Dogon culture, twins hold a deeply sacred role, embodying the duality and balance that is central to Dogon cosmology. For the Dogon people, the birth of twins is an event marked by spiritual significance, believed to be a blessing from the divine forces that govern the universe. Twins are seen as unique beings who represent a unity of opposites—male and female, light and dark, life and death—and their arrival into the world is considered a direct manifestation of cosmic principles. This sacred view of twins is deeply rooted in the Dogon belief in duality as the foundation of all existence, with each part of the world being balanced by an opposite, and each life force being mirrored by another. Twins are the physical representation of this duality, embodying the harmonious coexistence of two connected yet distinct forces.

The creation myth of the Dogon includes the Nommo, divine beings who were created in pairs by Amma, the supreme creator. The Nommo themselves were twin-like, embodying both male and female aspects, and were given the responsibility of guiding humanity and imparting sacred knowledge. The Dogon believe that human twins are connected to the Nommo, sharing a unique spiritual bond with these primordial beings. This connection to the Nommo not only elevates twins to a revered status but also signifies that they carry within them a part of the divine balance and wisdom that the

Nommo represent. As such, twins are considered to possess a special spiritual essence, one that links them to the origins of the universe and the principles of order that Amma established.

In Dogon culture, the birth of twins is seen as a momentous event that brings the family closer to the spiritual realm. The community views twins as intermediaries between the human and divine worlds, with their presence believed to bridge the physical and spiritual realms. When twins are born, the family and the community hold ceremonies to honor them, performing rituals that acknowledge their unique status and the blessings they bring. These rituals are designed to protect the twins and ensure that they grow under the guidance of the divine forces that are believed to watch over them. Offerings are made to Amma and the ancestors to express gratitude and to seek their continued blessings, as the arrival of twins is understood to be both a gift and a responsibility. Through these ceremonies, the Dogon affirm their respect for cosmic balance, viewing twins as the embodiment of the duality that sustains the world.

The special role of twins extends beyond their birth; they are thought to possess insights and abilities that are unique to their nature as two halves of a greater whole. Twins are believed to have a profound connection to each other, one that transcends ordinary sibling bonds. This connection is seen as mystical, a reflection of the divine duality they represent. The

Dogon interpret this bond as an indication of the unity that exists within the natural order, a reminder that opposites are interconnected and that true balance requires a harmonious relationship between distinct forces. Twins are thus revered not only for their unique identities but for the deep, invisible bond that unites them, a bond that is a microcosm of the balance found in the universe itself.

The Dogon celebrate this connection and honor the role of twins through various cultural practices and beliefs that reinforce the significance of duality in everyday life. Twins are often included in spiritual rituals and ceremonies, serving as symbols of the harmony that the Dogon strive to maintain within their community and their relationship with the environment. Their presence in these rituals is believed to enhance the community's connection to the divine, amplifying the spiritual power of the ceremonies and drawing the blessings of the ancestors. By honoring twins, the Dogon reaffirm their commitment to living in accordance with the principles of balance and respect that Amma established at the beginning of time. In this way, twins are seen as guiding figures, reminding the Dogon people of the importance of unity, cooperation, and the harmonious coexistence of opposites.

For the Dogon, the sacred role of twins also extends to their cultural understanding of the life cycle. The Dogon believe that life and death are interconnected, two aspects of the same cosmic cycle, and that twins embody this duality of existence. Twins are thought to hold a unique awareness of the cyclical nature of life, death, and rebirth, as their own bond reflects the interplay of forces that govern the universe. Through their presence, they serve as reminders that life is a journey guided by balance, where each phase of existence—birth, life, and death—is intrinsically linked to the others. This belief in twins as embodiments of the life cycle reinforces the Dogon's reverence for the interconnectedness of all things, teaching that each life is part of a greater whole and that each person's existence is woven into the fabric of the cosmos.

In Dogon society, the reverence for twins also influences social values, particularly in regard to family, cooperation, and mutual support. Twins are seen as examples of interdependence, showing how two individuals can complement and strengthen each other. This example serves as a model for the community, teaching that strength comes from unity and that each member of society plays an essential role in maintaining harmony. Twins are often celebrated in songs, stories, and art, their symbolic power woven into the cultural fabric as a reminder of the values that sustain the community. By honoring twins, the Dogon reinforce their belief in cooperation and collective responsibility, viewing each relationship as a manifestation of the unity that holds the world together.

The role of twins in Dogon mythology and culture is a profound expression of the Dogon's respect for duality, balance, and the interconnectedness of all life. Twins are not only family members but sacred beings who embody the cosmic principles that define Dogon existence. Their presence in the community, their bond with each other, and their connection to the divine all serve to remind the Dogon people of their place within a larger cosmic order, a world shaped by Amma and guided by the enduring forces of unity, respect, and spiritual harmony. Through their veneration of twins, the Dogon continue to honor the sacred balance that sustains their world, embracing the wisdom of their ancestors and the teachings of the Nommo, who first embodied these truths at the dawn of creation.

Chapter 6: The Symbols of Earth and Sky

In Dogon mythology, the symbols of Earth and Sky represent the foundational forces that shape the universe, embodying the duality, balance, and interconnectedness that are central to Dogon cosmology. Earth and Sky are not simply natural phenomena or separate realms; they are living, conscious entities whose relationship defines the structure of existence and influences every aspect of life. The Earth is viewed as a nurturing, maternal presence, a source of fertility, growth, and stability. In contrast, the Sky is associated with the divine, the mysterious, and the powerful, embodying the realm of spirits, ancestors, and celestial bodies. Together, Earth and Sky form a sacred union, symbolizing the interconnectedness of the physical and spiritual worlds and serving as a constant reminder of the harmony and balance that the Dogon people seek to uphold.

The Earth is seen as the great mother, a fertile and protective force that sustains life and provides a home for all beings. In Dogon thought, the Earth is imbued with ashe, the spiritual energy that flows through all things, animating the natural world and connecting humans to their environment. This maternal aspect of Earth is celebrated in Dogon agriculture, where farming is considered a sacred activity that fosters a reciprocal relationship between people and the land. Planting, harvesting, and caring for the soil are viewed as acts of respect and gratitude, gestures that honor the Earth's life-giving essence. For the Dogon, the Earth is not simply a resource to be exploited; it is a living entity to be cherished and protected, an extension of the self that must be nurtured to maintain balance in the world. This perspective reinforces the Dogon's deep respect for nature, as they understand that their survival depends on the health and fertility of the land.

In contrast, the Sky symbolizes the spiritual and celestial realms, a vast and dynamic presence associated with divine forces, wisdom, and cosmic order. The Sky is where Amma, the supreme creator, resides, and it is from this realm that Amma's influence flows into the world. The Dogon believe that the Sky is home to the stars, the sun, and the moon, each of which plays a vital role in guiding human life and maintaining the cycles of nature. The Sky represents not only the physical heavens but also the domain of the ancestors and the spirits, who watch over their descendants and influence the world below. By observing the movements of celestial bodies, the Dogon interpret divine messages and understand the rhythms of the universe, which they seek to mirror in their own lives. This connection to the Sky reinforces their belief in the continuity between the physical and spiritual worlds, as well as their place within a larger cosmic order.

The relationship between Earth and Sky is symbolized in Dogon culture through the interplay of rain and soil, elements that embody the life-giving union of these two realms. Rain, which falls from the Sky, is seen as a blessing, a gift from Amma and the ancestral spirits. When rain nourishes the Earth, it enables crops to grow and life to flourish, demonstrating the cooperation between Earth and Sky. In Dogon rituals, rain is often celebrated as a sign of divine favor and abundance, a reminder that the Sky's influence is essential for sustaining the Earth's fertility. The Earth, in turn, receives the rain and transforms it into nourishment for plants and animals, symbolizing receptivity, patience, and transformation. This relationship reflects the Dogon understanding of balance and reciprocity, as the Earth and Sky work together to sustain life, teaching the Dogon that harmony in their own relationships is equally essential for well-being and continuity.

The Earth and Sky are also deeply connected in Dogon spiritual practices, particularly through the veneration of ancestors. The Dogon believe that ancestral spirits dwell in both the Earth and the Sky, bridging the physical and spiritual worlds. Ancestors are thought to reside in the Sky, where they continue to watch over the living, guiding and protecting their descendants. However, their spirits remain connected to the Earth through rituals, offerings, and memorials, which the Dogon perform to honor them. By maintaining this relationship, the Dogon acknowledge the enduring presence of the ancestors, who link past, present, and future generations. This dual presence reinforces the idea that Earth and Sky are not separate but are intimately linked through the cycle of life and death, a cycle that the Dogon respect and celebrate as part of the natural order.

Dogon art and architecture reflect the symbols of Earth and Sky, using form and structure to express cosmological principles. In a Dogon village, the layout of homes, granaries, and communal spaces often mirrors the cosmic relationship between Earth and Sky. Buildings are constructed using clay from the Earth, symbolizing the human connection to the land, while the rooftops open toward the Sky, representing openness to divine guidance and cosmic wisdom. This architectural design reflects the Dogon belief that Earth and Sky are both sacred and that their interaction is essential for life and prosperity. By living within structures that embody these principles, the Dogon are constantly reminded of their place within the universe and their responsibility to uphold harmony with the world around them.

The symbolism of Earth and Sky is further reinforced in Dogon rituals, where masks and costumes depict animals, ancestors, and celestial forces. These symbols are integral to ceremonial dances, in which the Dogon embody the energies of Earth and Sky, seeking to invoke harmony and balance in their lives. When wearing these masks, dancers are believed to channel the spirit of the beings they represent, establishing a sacred connection between the human world and the forces of nature and cosmos. Through dance, song, and ritual, the Dogon actively participate in the relationship between Earth and Sky, honoring both realms as essential to their existence.

In Dogon cosmology, Earth and Sky are more than physical elements; they are expressions of the divine principles that sustain life and order in the universe. Each realm has its qualities, energies, and responsibilities, yet neither can exist without the other. The Earth provides stability, nurturing, and a foundation for life, while the Sky offers guidance, movement, and spiritual influence. By honoring both, the Dogon cultivate a worldview that respects the interconnectedness of all things, embracing the balance and unity that Amma intended for creation. Through their rituals, architecture, and everyday practices, the Dogon maintain a living relationship with Earth and Sky, celebrating the dual forces that shape their world and provide a sense of purpose, continuity, and spiritual harmony.

Chapter 7: Spirits of the Ancestors

In Dogon culture, the spirits of the ancestors hold a revered and enduring role, embodying the connection between the living and the spiritual realm, bridging the earthly world and the cosmos. The Dogon people believe that ancestors do not disappear after death but rather transform into spiritual presences that continue to influence and protect their descendants. The spirits of the ancestors are seen as guardians who watch over the family and community, guiding them and providing wisdom in times of need. Honoring these spirits is an integral part of Dogon life, as it maintains the bond with those who have passed on and reinforces the continuity between past and present. Through this veneration, the Dogon strengthen their ties to the traditions, knowledge, and legacy left by their forebears, viewing these spirits as an active force that sustains the moral and spiritual health of the community.

When a member of the Dogon community dies, their journey to becoming an ancestral spirit is supported by a series of complex and sacred rituals. These rituals, which include the *dama* ceremony, are performed to ensure that the deceased's spirit reaches the realm of the ancestors peacefully and gains the ability to watch over the living. The *dama* is a pivotal event that combines music, dance, and mask performances, involving the entire community in a collective act of respect, reverence, and transition. This ceremony is not only a time of mourning but also a celebration of the deceased's life, allowing their spirit to be integrated into the world of the ancestors. During the *dama*, elaborate masks are worn, each representing different aspects of the deceased's personality or the ancestral forces they are joining. The performers embody the spirits of both the newly deceased and ancient ancestors, reinforcing the bond between the living and those who have passed on. Through this collective expression, the Dogon seek to guide the soul safely to its spiritual resting place, where it can assume the role of a protective ancestor.

Once the spirit has joined the ancestral realm, it is believed to take on the responsibility of overseeing the well-being of the family and community. Ancestors are thought to offer guidance, protection, and blessings, particularly during crucial moments such as harvests, family ceremonies, and life transitions. Their presence is also invoked when facing challenges, as the Dogon believe that the wisdom of the ancestors provides insights into resolving conflicts, healing the sick, or addressing difficult decisions. The spirits of the ancestors are seen as deeply connected to the land and the natural cycles, which they continue to influence from the spiritual realm. They are viewed as part of the natural environment, their presence felt in the winds, rains, and growth of the crops, reinforcing the belief that life is an interconnected system that includes both the living and the dead. This worldview underscores the Dogon's respect for nature, as they believe that honoring the ancestors also means honoring the land and its resources.

To maintain a harmonious relationship with the spirits of the ancestors, the Dogon perform regular rituals, offerings, and prayers at shrines dedicated to these spirits. These shrines serve as sacred spaces where the living can communicate directly with the ancestors, offering food, drink, and other symbolic items that demonstrate their gratitude and respect. By making these offerings, the Dogon reinforce their commitment to their heritage and seek the ancestors' blessings for protection, fertility, and prosperity. These practices are not just acts of devotion but also acts of responsibility, as maintaining the ancestral bond is seen as essential for the community's spiritual health and cohesion. The Dogon view the ancestors as guardians of tradition, morality, and social unity, believing that the ancestors' approval is necessary to ensure harmony within the family and the broader community. The ongoing communication with the spirits sustains the ancestral legacy, keeping it alive within the fabric of daily life and reinforcing the Dogon's collective identity.

The role of the ancestors extends into the upbringing of younger generations, as they are considered the custodians of wisdom, values, and cultural knowledge. Dogon children are taught to respect and honor their ancestors from an early age, learning that these spirits are always present, guiding them and ensuring their welfare. The ancestors are seen as teachers, their influence extending into the values of respect, responsibility, and cooperation. Through stories, rituals, and daily observances, the young learn that they are part of a lineage that connects them to their ancestors, creating a sense of identity and continuity that shapes their worldview. As they grow, children are gradually introduced to more complex spiritual teachings, deepening their understanding of the ancestral connection and preparing them to one day take on the responsibility of honoring and communicating with the spirits of the departed.

In Dogon ceremonies, the spirits of the ancestors are often symbolized through masks, sculptures, and ritual objects that capture their presence and power. These representations are more than artistic expressions; they are seen as vessels that allow the spirits to interact with the living. During sacred dances and gatherings, the Dogon wear masks that embody the ancestors, channeling their wisdom and influence. This ritual use of masks serves as a form of communication, allowing the community to receive the ancestors' blessings and guidance. The belief that the ancestors inhabit these masks during ceremonies creates a direct line of connection, a moment in which the boundaries between the physical and spiritual realms dissolve. Through these interactions, the Dogon reinforce the closeness of their relationship with the ancestors, reaffirming the sense of unity that binds them across time.

The spirits of the ancestors also serve as moral overseers, watching over the community and ensuring that cultural and ethical standards are upheld. The Dogon believe that the ancestors are deeply invested in the actions of the living and that they bless those who uphold the community's values while withdrawing support from those who act harmfully or selfishly. By living in accordance with the ancestors' teachings, the Dogon people seek to earn their blessings and avoid misfortune, understanding that ancestral favor is key to maintaining peace and prosperity. This belief reinforces social cohesion, as each member of the community is encouraged to act with integrity and respect, knowing that their actions reflect upon the entire lineage. Through their role as protectors, teachers, and moral guides, the spirits of the ancestors maintain a powerful influence, ensuring that Dogon culture and values endure across generations, creating a living legacy that keeps the community connected to its origins and grounded in its traditions.

Chapter 8: Rituals of Fertility and Harvest

In Dogon culture, the rituals of fertility and harvest are sacred practices that celebrate the natural cycles of life, growth, and renewal. These rituals are central to Dogon spirituality and serve as a means of honoring the Earth, invoking blessings from ancestral spirits, and seeking the favor of divine forces to ensure abundance. For the Dogon, fertility and harvest are not merely agricultural events; they are deeply spiritual processes that require cooperation and harmony between the physical and spiritual worlds. Each season's planting and harvesting is an occasion to express gratitude to the Earth and the Sky, which the Dogon regard as living entities that work together to sustain all forms of life. Through their rituals, the Dogon reinforce their connection to nature, recognizing the land's sacred role in their survival and prosperity.

Fertility rituals are performed at the beginning of the growing season, when seeds are sown, and hope for a bountiful harvest takes root. These rituals are intended to prepare the soil and invoke divine favor, ensuring that the seeds planted will grow strong and yield abundant crops. The Dogon view the Earth as a maternal force, capable of nurturing life and providing sustenance. Fertility rituals often include offerings to the Earth, such as grains, seeds, and symbolic items that demonstrate respect and gratitude. These offerings are placed at shrines or sacred sites within the fields, marking the land as holy ground. Through these acts, the Dogon people seek to honor the Earth's life-giving power, acknowledging the land's role as a partner in their survival. The rituals often involve prayers and invocations to Amma, the supreme creator, asking for rain, fertility, and protection against drought or other natural adversities. These prayers express the community's faith in Amma's ability to guide and protect them, even as they strive to work in harmony with the cycles of nature.

Women play an essential role in fertility rituals, symbolizing their connection to the Earth and their capacity to bring forth life. In Dogon culture, women are regarded as custodians of fertility, and their participation in these ceremonies is believed to enhance the land's productive power. Their presence embodies the nurturing qualities of the Earth, as they engage in chants and dances that are intended to awaken the life force within the soil. Through rhythmic movements and ceremonial songs, the women invoke the spirits of fertility, calling upon them to bless the crops and ensure that the community will have enough food for the coming year. The Dogon believe that the energy channeled through these rituals helps to activate the Earth's potential, making it more receptive to the growth of plants. This ceremonial involvement strengthens the connection between the people and the land, creating a shared understanding that human life is intertwined with the health of the environment.

As the crops grow and reach maturity, the Dogon people continue to honor the spirits and forces of nature that sustain them. They observe the progress of their crops with reverence, celebrating each stage of growth as a manifestation of the Earth's blessings. The Dogon view the growth of plants as a sacred process that reflects the divine order established by Amma. They interpret the flourishing of their fields as a sign that their ancestors and deities are pleased with their efforts and dedication. By nurturing the crops with care, the Dogon maintain a relationship of respect and responsibility toward the land, understanding that their well-being depends on a reciprocal exchange with nature.

When the time for harvest arrives, it is celebrated with joyful ceremonies and communal gatherings. The harvest rituals are expressions of gratitude, as the Dogon give thanks for the abundance they have received and acknowledge the role of the Earth, ancestors, and divine beings in providing for their needs. These celebrations involve feasting, dancing, and singing, creating an atmosphere of unity and collective appreciation. The first harvested crops are offered to the spirits and ancestors, symbolizing the community's respect for those who came before and recognizing their continuing influence on the present. These offerings represent a gesture of humility and acknowledgment, reinforcing the belief that prosperity is a gift, not a guarantee. By giving a portion of their harvest to the spiritual realm, the Dogon reaffirm their understanding that all life is interconnected, and that human efforts alone are not sufficient to secure survival.

During the harvest festival, the Dogon also perform rituals to strengthen communal bonds, understanding that the Earth's gifts are meant to be shared among all. Elders lead these ceremonies, imparting wisdom and reinforcing the values of cooperation, generosity, and collective responsibility. The act of sharing the harvest serves as a reminder that individual prosperity is tied to the well-being of the community. By coming together in celebration, the Dogon express their gratitude for each other and for the support of the ancestors, whose guidance and protection are believed to contribute to the community's success. This collective gathering creates a sense of solidarity, reinforcing the importance of unity in both times of abundance and challenge.

The role of ancestors in these rituals is significant, as the Dogon believe that their presence and blessings are essential for a successful harvest. The ancestors are considered protectors of the land, ensuring that the community has the resources it needs to thrive. By honoring them during the harvest, the Dogon acknowledge their dependence on ancestral wisdom and strength, recognizing that each generation builds upon the legacy of those who came before. The ancestors are viewed as part of the natural cycles, their spirits connected to the land, water, and sky. This belief in the ancestors' enduring influence underscores the

Dogon's respect for continuity and tradition, reinforcing their commitment to preserving the values and practices that have sustained their community for centuries.

Through these fertility and harvest rituals, the Dogon people maintain a harmonious relationship with the land, their ancestors, and the divine forces that govern existence. Each planting and harvest season becomes a renewal of faith, a reminder of the interconnectedness of all life, and a testament to the community's dedication to honoring the sacred balance of the world around them. These rituals embody the Dogon's belief in the cyclical nature of life and their responsibility to care for the environment, ensuring that future generations will inherit a world that is as fertile, abundant, and spiritually rich as the one they now cherish.

Chapter 9: Masks, Dances, and Divine Communication

In Dogon culture, masks, dances, and rituals are not merely forms of art or entertainment; they are sacred conduits for communication with the divine and a means of maintaining harmony between the earthly and spiritual realms. These rituals allow the Dogon people to engage directly with spiritual forces, ancestors, and deities, bridging the visible and invisible worlds. Each mask, movement, and song within Dogon ceremonial practice is filled with symbolism, carrying messages of reverence, protection, and guidance. The Dogon believe that, through these rituals, they can invoke the presence of their ancestors and the spirits that oversee natural and cosmic orders, reinforcing their connection to the divine forces that shape their world.

Masks hold a unique significance in Dogon rituals, as they are believed to be vessels for ancestral and spiritual energies. Carved with skill and infused with intention, each mask represents a specific ancestor, spirit, or natural force, giving form to the unseen. These masks are crafted by skilled artisans who understand both the physical craft and the spiritual purpose of their work, creating pieces that are not just beautiful but spiritually powerful. For the Dogon, a mask is more than an object; it is a living entity that embodies the spirit it represents. The mask becomes a channel through which the spiritual world interacts with the physical, allowing the wearer to become a vessel for divine communication. Each mask has a distinct purpose and story, from representing the primordial beings, the Nommo, to embodying animals, elements, and ancestral spirits that influence life in all its aspects. The Dogon believe that by wearing these masks, they invite the spirits to participate in their ceremonies, receiving blessings, guidance, and protection.

Dances performed with these masks are an essential part of the Dogon's spiritual life, as they bring the masks to life and convey the sacred messages embedded within each gesture. The dancers are not simply performers but participants in a sacred ritual, entering into a state of connection with the spiritual forces represented by the masks. The movements are deliberate and meaningful, each step, posture, and rhythm communicating specific ideas about balance, unity, and the flow of life. Some dances mimic the movements of animals, while others represent the forces of nature or celestial cycles, reflecting the Dogon understanding of harmony within the universe. By embodying these forces, the dancers help their community remember the spiritual relationships that sustain them and celebrate the connection between the natural world and human existence. The dances serve as a reminder of the values of balance and respect, principles that are central to Dogon cosmology and cultural identity.

One of the most important ceremonies where masks and dances play a central role is the *dama*, a ritual held to honor and guide the spirits of the deceased into the ancestral realm. During the *dama*, dancers wear a series of masks that represent both the living and the dead, each mask embodying a unique aspect of the human experience and the spiritual journey after death. The *dama* is both a farewell to the departed and a renewal of the community's spiritual ties, reinforcing the belief that life continues beyond death and that the ancestors remain an integral part of the community's strength and wisdom. Through the ritual dances of the *dama*, the Dogon believe they are guiding the souls of the deceased to their final resting place, ensuring that these spirits can join the realm of the ancestors and watch over the living with protection and favor.

The presence of masks and dances in these ceremonies serves not only to honor the deceased but also to renew the community's relationship with the spiritual world, a bond that the Dogon believe is essential for prosperity, harmony, and protection. Masks worn during ceremonies are often large, elaborate, and highly symbolic, some even extending several feet above the dancer's head, representing the reach of the spiritual realm into the human world. The dancers' movements are designed to bring forth the spirit of the mask, channeling the ancestral energies that are believed to oversee the well-being of the community. In these moments, the dancers are no longer themselves but are transformed into vessels of divine energy, embodying the spirits they represent. The Dogon people understand this as a sacred responsibility, with each dancer holding the role of mediator, allowing the community to communicate with forces that are beyond ordinary human understanding.

Beyond the *dama*, masks and dances are used in other rituals to invoke rain, ensure fertility, or celebrate successful harvests, each ritual a form of prayer expressed through movement and sound. The Dogon believe that these rituals can influence the natural world, encouraging the spirits to bring favorable conditions and sustain the cycles of growth and renewal. For instance, during droughts or times of poor harvest, the Dogon perform dances dedicated to rain spirits, wearing masks that represent water animals or ancestral figures associated with fertility. These dances are an expression of hope, faith, and connection to the divine forces that govern natural cycles, underscoring the Dogon belief that human life is intricately linked to the rhythms of nature. By enacting these rituals, the Dogon affirm their commitment to living in harmony with the land, respecting its gifts, and recognizing their dependence on spiritual support for survival.

The presence of masks and dances in Dogon culture also serves as a means of education, particularly for younger generations. Through observation and participation in these ceremonies, young people learn the stories, values, and symbols that are central to their identity and spiritual understanding. The masks and dances are vehicles for passing down ancestral wisdom, providing a means of connection to the past and a guide for the future. In this way, the rituals ensure that each generation carries forward the knowledge of their culture, maintaining the community's continuity and respect for its origins. The dances and masks teach the importance of reverence for the ancestors, respect for the environment, and the need to uphold balance in all aspects of life, values that shape Dogon society and strengthen its cohesion.

For the Dogon, masks and dances are an irreplaceable form of divine communication, a means of bridging the physical and spiritual worlds. Through these rituals, the Dogon honor their ancestors, invoke blessings, and express their gratitude and respect for the forces that shape their lives. In each mask, each dance, and each beat of the drum, the Dogon see reflections of the divine, reminders of their place within the universe, and expressions of the principles that guide their way of life. These sacred practices continue to be a powerful source of spiritual sustenance, a living tradition that keeps the Dogon connected to their roots, their beliefs, and the cosmic forces that have shaped their world since the beginning of time.

Chapter 10: The Dogon Mysteries and Modern Fascination

The Dogon people of Mali have long captured the imagination of scholars, researchers, and spiritual seekers alike due to their rich mythology, intricate cosmology, and profound understanding of the natural and celestial worlds. One of the most captivating elements of Dogon knowledge is their precise understanding of the Sirius star system, particularly their awareness of Sirius B, a small, dense white dwarf star that is invisible to the naked eye. According to Dogon tradition, they have held knowledge of Sirius B for centuries, describing it as a small yet extremely heavy star that orbits Sirius A in a fifty-year cycle, a fact that modern astronomers only confirmed with advanced telescopic technology in the 20th century. The Dogon claim that this knowledge was imparted by the Nommo, amphibious beings sent by Amma, the supreme creator, who descended to Earth from the Sirius star system to share their wisdom and guidance. The idea that such detailed astronomical information could be embedded in an ancient oral tradition has led to widespread intrigue and speculation, sparking questions about the origins of Dogon knowledge and their possible connections to extraterrestrial or ancient advanced civilizations. This fascination with the Dogon mysteries was brought to global attention through the work of French anthropologists Marcel Griaule and Germaine Dieterlen, who spent years studying Dogon culture and cosmology. In the mid-20th century, their findings revealed that the Dogon possessed sophisticated astronomical knowledge, including the existence of Sirius B, its orbit, and its relationship to Sirius A. These revelations stirred curiosity beyond the fields of anthropology and ethnography, crossing into the realms of astronomy, ancient history, and even speculative theories about extraterrestrial life. The idea that a remote, indigenous community in West Africa could know details about a star that cannot be seen without modern technology has led to various theories about the sources of Dogon wisdom, with some researchers suggesting that the Dogon could have received knowledge from ancient visitors from other worlds or inherited it from a forgotten advanced civilization. While these theories are often speculative, they reflect the global intrigue that has surrounded the Dogon's knowledge and the broader mysteries of their mythology.

However, scholars who study the Dogon caution against taking these mysteries solely at face value or interpreting them through modern scientific frameworks. The Dogon's knowledge of the stars is deeply embedded in their spiritual beliefs and cosmological narratives, where Sirius and the Nommo play critical roles in the creation and balance of the universe. The Dogon do not view Sirius B as merely an astronomical object; rather, it is a symbol of order, rhythm, and divine connection, representing the guiding influence of the Nommo and the cosmic principles established by Amma. For the Dogon, knowledge is both physical and spiritual, intricately connected to their understanding of life, nature, and the universe's invisible forces. While modern science may focus on the material aspects of their astronomical knowledge, the Dogon perspective emphasizes the unity of physical observation with spiritual insight, highlighting a worldview that perceives the cosmos as a living, interrelated whole.

This blend of science and spirituality has made Dogon cosmology especially intriguing to contemporary thinkers seeking alternative ways to understand existence and the human relationship to the universe. Many are drawn to the Dogon's integrated approach, which respects both the visible and invisible dimensions of life. For those interested in indigenous knowledge systems, the Dogon represent a powerful example of how ancient wisdom can coexist with, and even complement, modern scientific inquiry. Their understanding of ashe, the life force that flows through all beings, aligns with the notion that everything in the universe is interconnected, a concept that resonates with modern interests in holistic and ecological worldviews. As more people look for meaning beyond reductionist explanations of life, the Dogon's teachings offer a rich, expansive perspective that connects humanity with the larger rhythms of the cosmos, a perspective that sees knowledge as a sacred gift that links people, nature, and the stars.

Beyond their cosmology, the Dogon's rich mythology, rituals, and symbolic practices continue to captivate audiences. Their elaborate mask dances, which serve as a means of communicating with the divine, and their ancestral veneration practices are profound cultural expressions that have influenced artists, writers, and spiritual communities worldwide. The Dogon's use of masks and dances in rituals serves as a reminder of the sacredness of life and the importance of honoring forces beyond human understanding. These ceremonies are not just cultural artifacts but living expressions of the Dogon's connection to the invisible realms and their ancestors. This dimension of Dogon life has contributed to a fascination that extends beyond their knowledge of the stars, as it demonstrates a way of life where art, ritual, and spirituality are interwoven, offering lessons on the significance of community, reverence, and the sacred in human existence.

Yet, with this global fascination also comes the risk of misunderstanding and exoticizing Dogon culture, viewing their knowledge as isolated mysteries rather than appreciating it as part of a broader African tradition of cosmological thought. Often, interpretations of Dogon mythology have overemphasized the mystery of their knowledge without fully acknowledging the context in which it developed, where observation of the natural world and deep spiritual introspection shaped their worldview. The Dogon are sometimes portrayed as keepers of a "lost knowledge," but in reality, their understanding of the universe is part of a continuum of knowledge that has been preserved and passed down through generations. It is rooted in a way of life that values observation, reflection, and respect for both nature and the unseen forces believed to animate it. This respect for continuity and balance in life reflects the Dogon's philosophy, which holds that human life is part of a vast, interconnected system of relationships and energies.

The ongoing fascination with the Dogon mysteries speaks to humanity's timeless search for answers to the larger questions of existence, as well as a growing appreciation for indigenous ways of knowing that integrate spirituality with knowledge of the physical world. In a world often dominated by scientific perspectives that prioritize empirical observation, the Dogon offer an alternative view, one where the cosmos is not merely a collection of stars and planets but a living, dynamic entity connected to human destiny. Their teachings on balance, respect, and cosmic order resonate across cultures and time, reminding modern audiences that ancient knowledge carries wisdom that remains relevant today. As people continue to seek meaning in the stars and explore humanity's place within the universe, the Dogon provide a powerful example of how knowledge can bridge worlds, connecting the tangible with the transcendent, and bringing people closer to the mysteries that have shaped their lives for centuries.

BOOK 4
AKAN MYTHOLOGY
ANANSI'S WEB: STORIES AND DEITIES OF AKAN MYTHOLOGY
SAMUEL SHEPHERD

Chapter 1: Nyame, the Supreme Sky God

In Akan mythology, Nyame is the Supreme Sky God, the ultimate creator, ruler of the heavens, and the source of all life. Revered as an omnipotent and omniscient deity, Nyame occupies a central position in the Akan pantheon, representing both the boundless power of the universe and the nurturing, life-giving force that sustains all beings. Nyame is believed to have created not only the Earth and all its creatures but also the order and balance that govern existence. As the god of the sky, Nyame is associated with the sun, moon, stars, and the vast expanse of the heavens. His presence is seen in the cycles of day and night, the changing of seasons, and the rain that nurtures the Earth. Nyame's role in the natural world reflects his vast power and the belief that everything under the sky is touched by his influence.

Nyame is often depicted as a remote yet benevolent deity, one who does not intervene directly in the daily lives of humans but remains an all-encompassing presence. His vastness is symbolized by the endless sky, which spans the earth and touches everything beneath it. This quality of transcendence sets Nyame apart from other deities in the Akan belief system, many of whom are more directly involved in human affairs. However, Nyame's distance does not diminish his importance; instead, it reinforces his role as a supreme being who is beyond the reach of mortal concerns, embodying a cosmic perspective that encompasses the whole of creation. His power is absolute, and he governs the other gods, or *abosom*, who are considered his children and who serve as intermediaries between Nyame and humanity. These *abosom* embody various aspects of the natural world—such as rivers, mountains, and forests—and assist Nyame in the maintenance of universal order by overseeing specific domains and responding to the needs of the people.

The Akan people believe that Nyame created the first humans, endowing them with life and a connection to the Earth. The breath of life, considered a gift from Nyame, is what animates each individual, binding them to the cosmos and linking them to the divine source. This belief establishes a sacred bond between humanity and Nyame, with each life seen as a manifestation of his creative power. Nyame is also credited with imparting wisdom and moral order, offering guidance to the ancestors and passing down teachings that became the foundation of Akan ethics and community life. Nyame's teachings emphasize the importance of respect, balance, and harmony, values that are integral to the Akan way of life. Through Nyame's influence, the Akan people are reminded of their responsibility to live with integrity, honor the environment, and uphold justice within their communities.

Although Nyame is distant, he is not inaccessible; the Akan people communicate with him through prayer, offerings, and rituals, seeking his blessings, guidance, and protection. These rituals are often performed with the assistance of the *abosom*, who are seen as closer to the human realm and more attuned to the needs of individuals and communities. By honoring the *abosom*, the Akan people believe they are also honoring Nyame, as these lesser gods are expressions of his divine will and extensions of his power. The *abosom* act as mediators, bridging the gap between the Supreme Sky God and humanity, carrying prayers to Nyame and delivering his blessings to the people. In this way, Nyame's presence is felt in everyday life, even if he remains in the distant sky.

Rain, one of the most essential gifts from Nyame, is especially significant in Akan mythology and is seen as a blessing directly from the Sky God. The Akan people believe that rain is a manifestation of Nyame's benevolence and a symbol of his nurturing power. Rain brings fertility to the land, sustains crops, and supports life, reinforcing the bond between Nyame and the Earth. During times of drought, the Akan perform rituals to appeal to Nyame, offering prayers and sacrifices in hopes of receiving rain. These rituals highlight the Akan's dependence on Nyame's favor for their survival and well-being, as well as their gratitude for the life-giving water that flows from the sky. The act of praying for rain is more than a request for sustenance; it is an acknowledgment of Nyame's role as the provider of all things and a reaffirmation of the sacred relationship between humanity and the divine.

The Akan also attribute the sun and moon to Nyame's celestial powers, each symbolizing different aspects of his influence over the world. The sun, which provides warmth and light, represents Nyame's life-giving and sustaining qualities, illuminating the path for both humans and the natural world. The moon, with its cycles and phases, is seen as a symbol of time, change, and the cyclical nature of existence, reflecting Nyame's role in governing the rhythms of life. Together, the sun and moon serve as reminders of Nyame's omnipresence and his control over the passage of time, with their movements marking the days, months, and seasons that structure human life. Through the sun and moon, the Akan people are constantly aware of Nyame's influence, understanding that each day and night is a reflection of his divine order.

Nyame's role in Akan society extends to their understanding of life and death, as he is seen as both the giver of life and the one who welcomes souls after death. The Akan believe that upon passing, each person's spirit returns to Nyame, completing the cycle of existence and reuniting with the divine source. This belief instills a sense of continuity and eternal connection to Nyame, as every soul is thought to originate from him and eventually returns to him. This cyclical view of life reinforces the importance of living in accordance with Nyame's teachings, as the soul's journey is shaped by the values it upheld in life. Through honoring Nyame, the Akan people celebrate life, death, and rebirth as stages in a journey that is both individual and universal, guided by the principles of respect, gratitude, and harmony that Nyame embodies.

In Akan mythology, Nyame is both a remote creator and an intimate presence, his essence woven into the fabric of existence. He is worshiped as the ultimate protector, the source of justice, and the guardian of order, governing the natural and spiritual worlds through his wisdom and power. His role in the Akan belief system underscores the idea that humanity is connected to the cosmos, each life a reflection of a larger, divine plan. By respecting and honoring Nyame, the Akan people align themselves with this plan, acknowledging that their lives are part of a vast, interwoven universe. Nyame's influence reaches across the heavens and Earth, touching every part of life, from the nurturing rains to the blazing sun, guiding his people to live in harmony with each other, with nature, and with the unseen forces that shape their existence.

Chapter 2: The Creation of the World

In many African mythologies, the creation of the world is a story filled with power, purpose, and profound meaning. Among the Akan people, creation begins with the supreme god Nyame, the Great Sky God, who is both distant and omnipresent, watching over the cosmos and guiding its intricate unfolding. Before there was life, light, or form, there was Nyame, who existed alone in a vast, boundless void. Within this vastness, he held all possibilities, embodying both the potential and energy needed to bring forth existence. Nyame decided to create the world, initiating a process that would transform the emptiness into a realm filled with life, motion, and meaning. By his will, Nyame gave shape to the heavens and the Earth, establishing the foundations upon which life could flourish. His act of creation was not only physical but also spiritual, giving each part of the cosmos a purpose and role within an interconnected whole.

Nyame's first act was to divide the heavens from the Earth, creating a space where life could exist separately from his celestial domain. By establishing the Earth as a distinct realm, Nyame set the stage for a universe that would thrive with diversity, order, and balance. He filled the heavens with the sun, moon, and stars, each celestial body a symbol of his divine power and a guide for the rhythms of life. The sun, representing warmth and life, would illuminate the world by day, while the moon, a symbol of change and cycles, would watch over the night, marking the passage of time. In creating the celestial bodies, Nyame established the cycles that would govern life on Earth, ensuring that each day and season brought new energy and growth.

Having shaped the heavens, Nyame then turned his attention to the Earth, transforming it from a barren, lifeless landscape into a world capable of supporting an abundance of life. He created the mountains, valleys, rivers, and forests, shaping a land that would provide for all beings. Each part of the Earth was crafted with care, intended to serve a specific purpose in the ecosystem Nyame envisioned. The rivers would bring water to nourish the land, the forests would shelter animals, and the fertile soil would support plants and crops, providing sustenance for the beings that would soon inhabit this world. By breathing life into the Earth itself, Nyame endowed it with a spirit, a connection to the divine that would allow humans and nature to live in harmony, drawing upon the energy of the land while respecting its sacredness.

Nyame's creation extended to the animals, plants, and humans, each group given distinct qualities and responsibilities within the grand design of life. The animals were created first, each one given specific abilities to navigate and thrive within its environment. Birds took to the skies, symbolizing the connection between Earth and the divine realm, while fish filled the rivers and oceans, symbolizing abundance and adaptation. By granting these animals their unique qualities, Nyame ensured that each would contribute to the balance and order of the natural world. Following the animals, Nyame brought forth the plants, which would feed the animals, enrich the soil, and provide beauty and diversity to the landscape. Plants were seen as life-giving entities, essential for maintaining the ecosystem and symbolizing growth, renewal, and resilience. Nyame's careful creation of each species reflected his intention to create a world that was both sustainable and interdependent, where every being had a role and every role contributed to the well-being of the whole.

Finally, Nyame created humans, whom he formed with special care, breathing into them a spark of his own divine spirit. This spark not only gave humans life but also endowed them with awareness, intelligence, and a unique connection to the divine. Humans were placed on Earth to tend to the land, care for the animals, and live in harmony with each other and the natural world. Nyame's gift of wisdom and creativity allowed humans to adapt, learn, and grow, with the capacity to make choices that would influence their destiny and the world around them. Nyame taught them to respect the cycles of nature, to honor the animals and plants as sacred parts of creation, and to recognize the interconnectedness that held all things together. Humans were thus entrusted with the responsibility to live in balance with the world, drawing upon the Earth's resources with gratitude and care.

The relationship between humans and the divine was further reinforced by the role of ancestors, who were believed to carry forward Nyame's teachings and wisdom, guiding each new generation. Ancestors held a revered position, as they were seen as the intermediaries between the living and Nyame, the guardians of knowledge and spiritual continuity. By honoring their ancestors, humans maintained their connection to the creator and showed respect for the legacy of life Nyame had set in motion. The wisdom of the ancestors reinforced the values of respect, harmony, and communal responsibility, which were central to maintaining the divine balance Nyame had established.

The creation of the world by Nyame was not only a physical act but a moral one, where each being was given a purpose within a framework of interdependence and respect. By giving life to the Earth and setting cycles in motion, Nyame established principles that would ensure the sustainability and harmony of his creation. His role as the creator also made him the ultimate guardian of justice, reminding humans that their actions must align with the cosmic order. The sun, moon, and stars became symbols of his watchful eye, reminders that all life operates under his guidance and within his divine design. The creation story of Nyame encapsulates the Akan belief in the sacredness of life, the interconnectedness of all beings, and the responsibilities that come with existence.

In this world shaped by Nyame, every part of nature is seen as a gift, and every act of life a tribute to the divine source. The creation of the world is, therefore, an ongoing process, where each cycle of growth, change, and renewal reflects the original act of creation. Through this story, the Akan people remember the sacred origins of their world, the values of respect and care, and the presence of Nyame in every aspect of life, from the earth beneath their feet to the heavens above.

Chapter 3: Asase Yaa: Mother Earth and Fertility

In Akan mythology, Asase Yaa is revered as the great Mother Earth, a powerful and nurturing deity who embodies fertility, life, and the very foundation upon which all existence rests. She is not just a god of the soil but is considered the essential force that sustains all living beings. Her name, often translated as "Old Woman Earth," reflects her ancient, enduring presence and her wisdom in supporting life through the cycles of birth, growth, death, and renewal. Asase Yaa is both the physical ground beneath people's feet and a spiritual entity, an ever-present reminder of the interconnectedness between humanity and nature. To the Akan people, she is the provider of sustenance, shelter, and abundance, and her presence infuses every part of the natural world with sacredness. She is seen in the richness of the soil, in the green of the trees, in the flowing rivers, and in the animals and plants that depend upon her.

As the goddess of fertility, Asase Yaa is central to agriculture and is honored each planting and harvest season as the source of life for crops and all that grows. Farmers pray to her for fertile soil and a bountiful harvest, believing that her blessing is essential for their survival. Before planting, they offer sacrifices to Asase Yaa, seeking her permission to disturb the earth and work its soil. These rituals underscore the Akan's belief that the land is not merely a resource but a living, sacred entity that deserves respect. By asking for Asase Yaa's blessing, the farmers acknowledge their dependence on her and their responsibility to treat the earth with reverence. The rituals of planting, caring for crops, and finally harvesting are seen as acts of partnership between the people and Asase Yaa, a recognition that human survival is bound to the health and generosity of the land.

Asase Yaa's association with fertility extends beyond agriculture, touching every aspect of life and creation. She is honored as the force behind childbirth and the cycle of human generations. Women, in particular, hold a strong connection to Asase Yaa, as she represents the nurturing and life-giving powers that are essential to motherhood. Pregnant women may pray to Asase Yaa for safe delivery and the health of their children, viewing her as a protector who watches over mothers and infants. The Akan people believe that Asase Yaa's blessing is present in each child born, each new generation a continuation of her life-giving energy. This close association with childbirth and family reinforces Asase Yaa's role as not only the provider of physical sustenance but also the guardian of lineage and community continuity. Just as the earth nurtures seeds into plants, so too does Asase Yaa nurture families, ensuring the survival and growth of her people.

The daily life of the Akan people is filled with practices and rituals that honor Asase Yaa's sacred role. It is customary to avoid disturbing the earth on certain days, particularly Thursdays, which are dedicated to her. On these days, farming, digging, and other activities that might disrupt the soil are halted out of respect, allowing the earth to rest. This practice, known as "Asase Yaa's day," reflects the belief that the land, like any living being, requires periods of rejuvenation. By observing these customs, the Akan demonstrate their respect for Asase Yaa and their understanding of balance, recognizing that their actions have a direct impact on the health of the land. This tradition also serves as a reminder that the earth's resources are not limitless and must be used responsibly. Asase Yaa's day is a time of reflection, a pause in the rhythm of life that allows people to honor the source of their sustenance and reconnect with the sacredness of the earth.

Asase Yaa is also seen as the final resting place for all beings. The Akan believe that, at death, each person returns to the earth, completing the cycle of life. Burials are conducted with great care and respect, as they represent a return to Asase Yaa's embrace. This view of death as a return to the earth emphasizes the Akan understanding of life as a cycle, with each generation emerging from and returning to Asase Yaa. She is thus not only the source of life but also the place of peace and rest in death. This understanding brings comfort, as it reinforces the idea that death is not an end but a transition back to the nurturing earth. By returning to Asase Yaa, individuals are believed to continue influencing and supporting the lives of their descendants, becoming part of the earth that nurtures future generations. The dead are buried with rituals that honor Asase Yaa, acknowledging her role in the eternal cycle of life, death, and rebirth.

The reverence for Asase Yaa reflects the Akan people's respect for nature and their belief in the interconnectedness of all things. Asase Yaa is present in every part of the land, from the fertile plains to the rugged mountains, and each aspect of the landscape is viewed as an expression of her power and presence. She is celebrated in songs, dances, and stories, her influence woven into the cultural and spiritual fabric of the Akan. Her image is often invoked in art and symbolism, reminding the community of her importance and the need to honor her with each passing season. Through these practices, the Akan maintain a close relationship with the earth, seeing themselves as custodians of a land that is not theirs to own but to care for, a gift from Asase Yaa that they must protect for future generations.

In Akan cosmology, Asase Yaa's role extends beyond the material, as she is also a force of moral and ethical guidance. Her nurturing and protective qualities inspire values of respect, care, and stewardship, urging people to treat each other and the land with kindness and responsibility. The Akan believe that to harm the earth is to harm oneself, for humans and the land are intertwined through Asase Yaa's life-giving power. This belief instills a profound sense of duty to protect the earth, to act as guardians of the natural world, and to preserve its resources. Through their reverence for Asase Yaa, the Akan people recognize the sacredness of life, understanding that all beings are connected by the cycles of growth, decay, and renewal that she oversees.

Chapter 4: Anansi the Spider: Trickster and Storyteller

Anansi the Spider is one of the most famous figures in Akan folklore, celebrated as both a trickster and a storyteller, a character whose wit and cleverness have captivated generations. Known for his cunning and resourcefulness, Anansi is often portrayed as a small yet intelligent spider who uses his mind to outwit larger, stronger creatures and to navigate the complexities of life. He is neither purely good nor entirely malicious; rather, he is a complex figure who embodies the nuanced realities of human nature, often blending wisdom with mischief in his pursuit of personal gain or to teach lessons to others. Anansi's tales are filled with humor, clever plots, and moral ambiguity, offering audiences insights into the strengths and flaws of human character and providing moral lessons on topics such as greed, generosity, cooperation, and resilience.

In Akan mythology, Anansi is more than just a character; he is a cultural hero who represents the power of storytelling and the wisdom that stories hold. Through his tales, Anansi reveals truths about life, often illustrating the importance of intelligence over brute strength, the value of perseverance, and the benefits of resourcefulness. His stories, known as *Anansesem*, are passed down orally from generation to generation, serving as both entertainment and instruction. These stories are told in family gatherings, around evening fires, and in communal spaces, binding communities together and reinforcing shared values. In each story, Anansi's adventures and schemes teach valuable lessons, and listeners learn through his actions about the consequences of pride, deceit, and hubris, as well as the rewards of cleverness, patience, and humility.

Anansi's role as a trickster is central to his character. Unlike traditional heroes who triumph through physical power or moral virtue, Anansi relies on his quick thinking and cunning nature to achieve his goals. His trickster qualities make him unpredictable, as he is willing to bend or break social rules if it means he can gain an advantage. In one story, Anansi tricks a group of powerful animals by feigning weakness and innocence, only to later exploit their trust for his benefit. Through this story, listeners are reminded that appearances can be deceiving and that underestimating others can lead to unexpected consequences. Anansi's ability to turn situations to his favor reflects a deep understanding of human psychology and social dynamics, as he uses both his knowledge of others and his quick wit to manipulate events to his advantage.

In addition to his trickster role, Anansi is also celebrated as the keeper and spreader of stories, earning him the title of "King of Stories." According to one legend, Anansi desired to possess all the world's stories, which were originally owned by Nyame, the Supreme Sky God. Determined to obtain them, Anansi approached Nyame and offered to buy the stories, only to be met with seemingly impossible tasks as conditions for the purchase. Nyame asked Anansi to capture dangerous creatures—the Leopard, the Hornet, and the Python—as a test of his bravery and cleverness. Undeterred, Anansi set out to complete each task, using his intelligence and cunning rather than force. Through a series of elaborate tricks, he successfully captured each creature, earning Nyame's admiration and ultimately being gifted the stories of the world. This tale underscores the importance of resilience, adaptability, and intelligence in overcoming obstacles, and it marks Anansi as a figure whose ambition and determination allow him to change the world.

As the "King of Stories," Anansi is tasked with sharing these stories, using his role as a storyteller to convey the wisdom and values of his culture. Anansi's tales often explore themes of survival and adaptation, resonating with audiences who recognize the challenges of life and the need for resilience in the face of adversity. Each story reveals a different aspect of human experience, from the struggle to find one's place in the world to the value of family and community. Anansi's stories are reflective, offering both amusement and insight as they challenge listeners to think critically about the world around them. His tales, filled with humor and irony, encourage people to question authority, challenge norms, and celebrate the diversity of human experience.

Anansi's legacy as a cultural figure extends beyond the Akan people and has spread across West Africa and into the Caribbean, the Americas, and beyond, brought by the African diaspora. In each region, Anansi's stories have evolved, taking on new forms and incorporating local elements, yet his essence remains the same: a figure who uses cleverness and humor to navigate life's challenges. In Caribbean folklore, for example, Anansi continues to be a symbol of resilience and adaptability, representing the spirit of survival among African descendants who faced oppression and hardship. His stories provided comfort and solidarity, embodying the idea that intelligence, laughter, and creativity could offer strength and resistance in difficult times. Through this transformation, Anansi became a symbol of resistance, hope, and the enduring power of storytelling, connecting generations across time and space through shared stories and values.

In each story, Anansi reflects the complexities of human nature, showing that cleverness and trickery can be both tools for survival and sources of conflict. Sometimes Anansi's schemes backfire, teaching him humility and restraint, while other times he emerges victorious, reminding listeners that even the smallest, most underestimated among us can achieve great things through intelligence and creativity. His multifaceted character invites audiences to reflect on their own choices, the boundaries of morality, and the consequences of ambition and greed. By embodying both flaws and virtues, Anansi provides a mirror for listeners, allowing them to explore their own identities and values within the safe space of a story.

Anansi the Spider remains a beloved figure, a trickster and storyteller who uses his wit to inspire, entertain, and educate. His tales are more than just stories; they are a cultural inheritance, a living tradition that celebrates the human spirit and the power of the mind. Through his actions, Anansi reminds us of the importance of creativity, resilience, and the stories that bind us together.

Chapter 5: Bia and Tano: Guardians of Nature

In Akan mythology, Bia and Tano are revered as powerful guardians of nature, embodying the protective and life-sustaining forces of the natural world. Bia, the god of the wilderness, and Tano, the river god, represent the untamed landscapes, fertile rivers, and ecosystems that support life. Together, they personify the elements of land and water, ensuring balance, abundance, and protection across the landscapes of the Akan people. Bia is often associated with the wild forests, mountains, and uncharted territories where he reigns as the guardian of all things untamed. He represents the raw power of the land, symbolizing both its beauty and its potential danger. To the Akan people, Bia embodies the spirit of the wilderness, a force that nurtures but can also fiercely protect itself against those who disrespect its sanctity. In the dense forests and rolling hills, Bia's presence is felt as a reminder of the deep, often mysterious bond between humanity and the natural world.

Tano, on the other hand, is the deity of rivers and freshwater sources, especially the mighty Tano River, which is named in his honor. He is the lifeblood of Akan society, providing water for drinking, farming, and sustaining the diverse flora and fauna that thrive along the riverbanks. Tano is viewed as a benevolent yet powerful force, a god whose flowing waters bring life and prosperity to the land. His rivers are seen as veins that connect communities, nourishing crops, filling streams, and supporting the ecosystem upon which the Akan people depend. But just as Tano's waters are essential for life, they can also be fierce and unforgiving. During times of heavy rain or floods, the river's force reminds people of Tano's strength and the importance of respecting natural boundaries. This duality—nurturing and formidable—underscores Tano's role as a god who both provides and demands respect for the waters he governs.

In Akan communities, both Bia and Tano are honored through rituals, offerings, and observances that reflect the people's dependence on nature and their respect for the forces that govern it. These rituals are carried out to seek blessings for the land and water, to express gratitude for their abundance, and to ask for protection against natural disasters. Farmers, hunters, and fishermen often make offerings to Bia and Tano, recognizing their roles as stewards of the wilderness and rivers. By doing so, the Akan people uphold a relationship of mutual respect and responsibility, understanding that their survival depends on the health and harmony of nature. These offerings include food, drink, and other symbolic items placed at sacred sites along rivers, near forest edges, or at shrines dedicated to these gods. Through these acts, the Akan people demonstrate their respect for the land and water as living entities, reinforcing the belief that nature is sacred and should be approached with humility.

The influence of Bia and Tano extends beyond their individual domains, shaping the moral and ethical views of the Akan people. Bia, as the god of the wild, teaches respect for boundaries, caution, and an understanding of nature's raw power. His wilderness is a place of beauty, but it is also one where carelessness can lead to misfortune. The Akan believe that Bia watches over hunters and travelers, ensuring that only those who enter the forest with respect and reverence are safe from harm. Hunters often perform rituals before entering the forest, asking Bia's permission to take from his domain and promising to act responsibly. In return, they hope to gain his protection and guidance, knowing that Bia's favor can mean the difference between success and danger. This reverence for Bia's territory instills a sense of responsibility in the Akan people, reminding them to take only what they need and to leave nature undisturbed whenever possible.

Tano, the river god, teaches the values of generosity, sustenance, and the cyclical nature of life. Just as the river waters return through rain and replenish the land, Tano's presence reminds the Akan of the interconnectedness of all life. His rivers sustain crops, feed animals, and support entire communities, embodying the idea that nature's resources are gifts meant to be shared. Fishermen and farmers honor Tano through ceremonies and offerings before they draw from the river's bounty, acknowledging his role in providing sustenance. Yet, Tano's might during floods or droughts serves as a reminder of the delicate balance that must be maintained with nature. The Akan people understand that taking too much or failing to honor Tano's gifts can lead to hardship, reinforcing the importance of gratitude, respect, and moderation in the use of natural resources.

Bia and Tano also symbolize the balance between land and water, wild and cultivated, individual and community. The Akan believe that both gods work in tandem, maintaining the harmony that allows life to thrive. Just as Bia's forests provide habitats for animals and plants, Tano's rivers connect these lands, supporting an ecosystem that reflects the unity of their roles. This connection between Bia and Tano serves as a metaphor for the Akan view of life, where each element of nature plays an essential part in sustaining the whole. By respecting both the forests and the rivers, the Akan people honor the balance that Bia and Tano represent, a balance that sustains life and ensures that future generations will continue to benefit from the gifts of nature.

The teachings of Bia and Tano permeate Akan cultural values, promoting conservation, respect, and coexistence. Through the reverence for these gods, the Akan people learn to live in harmony with their environment, to view the land and water as sacred, and to understand the need for stewardship in their daily lives. Bia and Tano embody the wisdom of nature, reminding humanity of its role as a part of the larger ecosystem and of the need to uphold the balance that allows all life to flourish. Through stories, rituals, and daily practices, the legacy of Bia and Tano endures, continuing to guide the Akan people in their relationship with the natural world, instilling values that reflect both respect for the earth and the understanding that humanity's fate is intertwined with the fate of the forests and rivers that sustain it.

Chapter 6: Spirits of the Forest and River

In Akan cosmology, the spirits of the forest and river are essential guardians of the natural world, embodying the powerful forces within trees, plants, rivers, and streams. These spirits, known as *asunsum* in Akan culture, are seen as protective entities that safeguard the health and balance of their respective domains, ensuring that nature's resources are treated with respect and care. The Akan people believe that every tree, rock, and body of water possesses a unique spirit, a living presence that embodies the sacredness of the environment. These spirits are not merely symbolic but are considered real forces that hold both the power to protect and the ability to punish those who exploit or disrespect nature. The forest and river spirits are deeply woven into the daily lives, traditions, and rituals of the Akan people, serving as constant reminders of the interconnectedness between humanity and the environment.

The spirits of the forest are often associated with specific trees, groves, and plants, each carrying its own spiritual significance and role within the ecosystem. The forest is seen as a sacred space, a place where these spirits dwell and where humans must tread carefully, aware of the unseen forces that guard the trees and wildlife. Some trees are considered especially sacred and are believed to be the homes of powerful spirits who watch over the forest and its creatures. These tree spirits are revered as protectors, embodying the strength, resilience, and endurance of the natural world. They are guardians of the forest's harmony, ensuring that the balance of life within its depths remains undisturbed. For this reason, trees in certain areas may not be cut or harmed without special permission and rituals to appease the spirits. Hunters, herbalists, and others who venture into the forest perform ceremonies to show respect to the spirits, asking for safe passage and success in their endeavors. This practice reinforces the belief that the forest is not a resource to be exploited but a living community deserving reverence and care.

Similarly, the spirits of the river embody the life-sustaining power of water, an element essential for both the land and the people. Rivers, streams, and lakes are seen as sacred spaces inhabited by these spirits, whose presence nourishes the land and supports life. The Akan people believe that rivers are more than just bodies of water; they are inhabited by spirits who govern the flow of life, fertility, and abundance. These river spirits are known for their nurturing qualities, as they provide water for drinking, farming, and supporting the ecosystem. However, they are also known for their strength and can become fierce if the river is disrespected or polluted. For the Akan, the act of polluting a river is not only an offense against the physical environment but an affront to the spirits who dwell within it. Such actions are believed to disrupt the spiritual balance and bring misfortune upon the community. To maintain harmony, the Akan people observe practices that protect the purity of rivers, honoring the spirits by avoiding waste, performing cleansing rituals, and making offerings at sacred water sites.

Both forest and river spirits play vital roles in the Akan understanding of health and well-being, as they are believed to influence not only the physical landscape but also the health of the human community. Herbalists and healers, who often work with plants, roots, and water, seek the blessings of the spirits when collecting herbs and other natural resources for medicinal purposes. They believe that by respecting these spirits, the medicine they create will be more effective, infused with the life force that the spirits impart. This practice emphasizes that healing is not merely a physical process but a spiritual one, requiring harmony with nature and acknowledgment of the spirits who provide these resources. Through rituals and offerings, healers express their gratitude and recognize that the power of their medicines comes not only from the physical properties of plants but from the spirits who dwell within them.

The spirits of the forest and river are also invoked during times of drought, illness, or hardship, as the Akan people seek their guidance and assistance. When the land suffers from a lack of rain, rituals may be performed at riverbanks, where offerings are made to appease the spirits and request rainfall to replenish the earth. During these rituals, community members gather to pray, chant, and pour libations, showing their respect for the spirits and acknowledging their dependence on the river's life-giving waters. The Akan believe that by honoring the spirits, they can restore balance to the natural world, bringing rain, health, and abundance back to the community. Such rituals reflect the Akan's understanding that the relationship with the spirits is reciprocal, requiring respect, gratitude, and mindfulness of nature's needs.

In Akan tradition, these spirits are also considered guardians of moral and ethical standards, with their presence reinforcing the values of respect, humility, and stewardship. Those who show disregard for the spirits, whether by harming the forest, polluting the rivers, or overusing resources, are believed to bring misfortune upon themselves and their communities. The spirits are seen as upholding a natural justice system, one in which nature itself responds to human actions. This belief instills a sense of accountability, as individuals and communities understand that their behavior directly impacts their relationship with the spirits and, by extension, their own well-being. By honoring the spirits and maintaining respectful practices, the Akan ensure the continued health of the forest, rivers, and, ultimately, their own lives.

The presence of these spirits in the Akan worldview highlights the belief in an interconnected, living universe, where humanity is part of a larger community that includes not only other people but also the environment and its unseen guardians. Stories and legends about encounters with forest and river spirits are passed down through generations, teaching children about the sacredness of nature and the values of care, respect, and gratitude. These stories serve as cultural guides, reminding the Akan people of their role as caretakers of the land and water. They are not simply residents in nature but participants in a spiritual relationship that requires both reverence and responsibility.

In this belief system, the spirits of the forest and river are not distant or abstract entities; they are present in daily life, shaping how the Akan interact with their surroundings. Through rituals, offerings, and traditions, the Akan maintain a living connection to these spirits, honoring their roles as protectors of the natural world and understanding that the well-being of the land, water, and people are inseparable. This respect for the spirits fosters a sense of unity with nature, a bond that strengthens the community's identity and ensures that each generation understands the importance of safeguarding the environment and honoring the forces that sustain life.

Chapter 7: The Wisdom of Ancestral Spirits

In Akan culture, the wisdom of ancestral spirits is revered as a guiding force that shapes the lives of the living, connecting each generation with those who came before. These ancestral spirits are more than just memories; they are active, spiritual presences believed to watch over their descendants, offering guidance, protection, and wisdom. The Akan people view the ancestors as custodians of knowledge, values, and traditions, embodying the experiences and insights gained through lifetimes. The respect for ancestral spirits is deeply rooted in the belief that the spirits continue to exist in a realm that closely interacts with the physical world, influencing events, guiding decisions, and offering blessings to those who honor them. To the Akan, living in harmony with ancestral wisdom means honoring their legacy, preserving the culture, and ensuring that their values continue to guide daily life.

The relationship between the living and the ancestors is strengthened through rituals, prayers, and offerings made at family shrines or sacred places. By pouring libations and offering symbolic gifts, the Akan people express gratitude, seek the ancestors' blessings, and ask for guidance in matters ranging from personal struggles to community decisions. These offerings are more than mere tradition; they are acts of respect that acknowledge the ongoing presence of the ancestors and reinforce the bonds that connect each generation. In times of hardship, the living turn to these ancestral spirits for insight, believing that the ancestors, with their wisdom and experience, can provide solutions to present-day problems. This belief in the guidance of ancestral spirits helps foster a sense of continuity, as each generation knows they are part of an unbroken lineage that has faced challenges, overcome obstacles, and endured through resilience.

Ancestral wisdom is particularly important in guiding moral and ethical decisions within Akan society. The ancestors are viewed as protectors of moral values, and their memory serves as a reminder of the principles that hold the community together. People often reflect on ancestral wisdom when considering questions of right and wrong, understanding that the values of respect, honesty, and responsibility have been passed down through generations. By living according to these values, the Akan people honor the legacy of their ancestors, ensuring that the principles that have sustained the community endure. This respect for ancestral wisdom also promotes social harmony, as each member of the community is encouraged to act with integrity, knowing that their actions reflect not only on themselves but on their entire lineage.

In addition to moral guidance, the ancestral spirits are believed to hold profound knowledge about life, health, and nature. Healers, herbalists, and spiritual leaders frequently call upon the ancestors when seeking knowledge about traditional medicines and healing practices. It is believed that the ancestors have an intimate understanding of the natural world, a wisdom that was cultivated over generations and passed down to guide the living. This ancestral knowledge is woven into the practices of healing, agriculture, and community life, offering solutions that align with nature's rhythms and cycles. The healers may consult the ancestors in dreams, prayers, or meditative rituals, hoping to gain insight into remedies, treatments, and approaches that will aid those in need. This consultation with ancestral spirits reflects a holistic approach to health and well-being, one that respects the interconnectedness of body, spirit, and nature.

The wisdom of the ancestors also plays a significant role in governance and leadership within Akan society. Elders, who are seen as the living links to the ancestral world, hold positions of authority and respect, often making decisions with the guidance of ancestral teachings. When faced with important choices, leaders and elders may invoke the spirits of the ancestors, asking for their insight to ensure that the community's actions align with tradition and wisdom. This reliance on ancestral guidance reinforces the belief that the past holds valuable lessons for the present, and that the experiences of previous generations offer a foundation upon which the future can be built. By honoring the ancestors in leadership decisions, the Akan people maintain a strong connection to their heritage, fostering a sense of continuity that helps to unify the community.

In the Akan worldview, death is not an end but a transition into a spiritual realm where the ancestors continue to exist, watching over their descendants and guiding them through life's challenges. The deceased are remembered in regular ceremonies, festivals, and personal moments of reflection, as these acts of remembrance help to keep their presence alive. During special occasions, such as births, weddings, and other important milestones, the ancestors are invited to join in celebration, reinforcing the bond between the living and the departed. This continuous interaction with the spirits creates a sense of companionship, a feeling that the ancestors remain close, sharing in the joys and sorrows of their descendants. The belief in the presence of ancestral spirits brings comfort and reassurance, as it reminds people that they are never truly alone; the wisdom and strength of their ancestors are with them always.

The ancestral spirits also serve as a source of inspiration and resilience for the Akan people, who look to the past as a testament to the endurance and strength that runs through their lineage. When facing difficulties, individuals may find encouragement in the knowledge that their ancestors endured similar struggles and that they, too, can draw on this legacy of resilience. This perspective strengthens the Akan community, reinforcing the values of patience, perseverance, and unity. By seeing themselves as part of a long line of ancestors, individuals understand that their actions impact not only themselves but the generations that will follow. This sense of responsibility inspires them to make choices that honor the sacrifices of the past and contribute to the well-being of future descendants.

The wisdom of ancestral spirits is thus a foundation upon which the Akan way of life is built, shaping the community's beliefs, practices, and values. It influences how they interact with each other, how they care for the land, and how they face the challenges of life. By honoring the ancestors, the Akan people maintain a connection to a vast source of wisdom and guidance, one that has been preserved through stories, traditions, and rituals. In this way, ancestral spirits are woven into the very fabric of life, bridging the past and present and creating a cultural legacy that sustains the Akan people through every season, generation, and change. The presence of these spirits is a testament to the enduring power of heritage and the deep respect for the wisdom that the ancestors continue to impart, reminding each generation of the strength, insight, and unity that define their community.

Chapter 8: Myths of Justice and Morality

In Akan mythology, stories of justice and morality serve as essential teachings that guide the community's values, reinforcing a shared understanding of right and wrong. These myths are not merely tales of ancient events; they are powerful narratives that embody the ethical principles of the Akan people, illuminating the consequences of actions and the moral paths that individuals are encouraged to follow. Each story is crafted with a purpose, whether to illustrate the virtue of honesty, the dangers of greed, or the importance of humility. Through these myths, the Akan communicate the standards of justice and morality that bind the community together, teaching young and old alike the values that sustain social harmony and individual integrity.

One of the most well-known Akan myths of justice involves Anansi the Spider, the trickster figure who often embodies both cleverness and selfishness. In a particular story, Anansi tries to deceive other animals by tricking them into working for him without reward, hoping to hoard resources for himself. At first, Anansi appears to succeed, exploiting the trust of others and taking what he wants without sharing. However, as the story unfolds, Anansi's deceit is exposed, and he suffers the consequences of his actions, often through the cunning of others or by his own undoing. This myth reveals the Akan belief that deceit and exploitation cannot go unpunished and that those who manipulate others for personal gain will ultimately face justice. Anansi's downfall serves as a reminder to act fairly and honestly, encouraging listeners to value cooperation and respect over selfish ambition.

Another central theme in Akan myths of justice and morality is the importance of generosity and compassion, illustrated in stories that show the rewards of kindness and the perils of greed. In one such tale, a wealthy farmer hoards his crops during a time of famine, refusing to share with his hungry neighbors. When he finally decides to open his storehouses, he finds that his crops have rotted, leaving him with nothing. Meanwhile, a poor farmer who shared his meager harvest with those in need is blessed with abundance in the following season. This myth reflects the Akan understanding that generosity creates a cycle of blessings, while greed leads to misfortune. By sharing with others, individuals contribute to the well-being of the community and reinforce the bonds of solidarity that protect everyone. The Akan see such acts of compassion as essential to maintaining balance, a principle that is integral to the moral fabric of society.

Justice in Akan myths is also tied to the role of ancestors and spiritual forces, who are believed to oversee human actions and ensure accountability. The Akan believe that ancestral spirits, acting as guardians of morality, can influence the outcome of events, intervening when necessary to correct wrongdoing or to support those who uphold moral values. In one story, a young man falsely accuses an elder of theft to cover his own crime. Despite the lack of evidence, the elder is held accountable by the community, and his reputation is damaged. However, during a ritual to honor the ancestors, the truth is revealed, as the spirits expose the young man's deception. The elder's honor is restored, and the young man faces shame and punishment for his falsehoods. This story reflects the Akan belief that truth and justice will ultimately prevail, supported by the ancestors who watch over their descendants. Such myths reinforce the idea that actions have consequences not only in the physical world but in the spiritual realm as well, where the ancestors ensure that justice is served.

Akan myths also emphasize the importance of humility and respect, especially in relationships with elders, family members, and the community. One story tells of a boastful warrior who, believing himself to be invincible, disrespects a wise elder's advice and challenges the gods by claiming he has no need for their protection. In his pride, the warrior embarks on a journey alone, only to encounter forces beyond his control. Facing overwhelming odds, he realizes his limitations and learns that true strength lies in humility and respect for those who offer wisdom and guidance. This tale teaches the Akan value of humility, reminding individuals that arrogance can lead to downfall, and that wisdom often resides in those who have lived long and learned much. By respecting elders and honoring their guidance, the Akan believe that individuals can avoid pitfalls and live lives that contribute to the greater good.

Additionally, Akan myths often explore the theme of loyalty and trustworthiness, celebrating these qualities as pillars of strong relationships and a harmonious community. In one well-known tale, a close friendship is tested when one friend is accused of wrongdoing. Despite the mounting pressure to abandon him, the loyal friend remains by his side, even risking his own reputation to defend him. In the end, the friend's loyalty leads to the truth being revealed, proving the accused innocent and rewarding the loyalty that helped him. This myth underscores the importance of trust and loyalty, teaching that these values create bonds strong enough to withstand adversity. The Akan view loyalty as a sacred duty, a value that holds friendships, families, and communities together in times of challenge and conflict.

The Akan myths of justice and morality are more than cautionary tales; they serve as frameworks for understanding how to live in alignment with the community's principles. By passing down these stories, the Akan preserve a legacy of ethical teaching, ensuring that each generation understands the importance of living with integrity. The values highlighted in these myths—honesty, compassion, humility, and loyalty—shape the identity of the Akan people, reinforcing the belief that moral behavior is essential for individual and collective well-being. Through their storytelling, the Akan not only entertain but educate, instilling values that empower people to contribute positively to society and maintain a sense of justice and balance that resonates throughout their lives. In these myths, the Akan see their own experiences reflected and their ideals embodied, creating a powerful cultural heritage that guides them toward a just and moral life.

Chapter 9: Folktales of Wisdom and Cunning

Folktales of wisdom and cunning are central to Akan storytelling, capturing the resourcefulness, intelligence, and moral lessons that guide everyday life. In these stories, clever characters use wit and strategic thinking to overcome obstacles, solve problems, and navigate complex social situations. Often featuring animals as protagonists—most famously Anansi the Spider—these folktales entertain, educate, and reflect the cultural values of the Akan people. Anansi, the master of trickery and wit, frequently appears in these tales, embodying the idea that intelligence and adaptability can be just as powerful as physical strength. Through his adventures, Anansi demonstrates the value of keen observation, quick thinking, and creative problem-solving, characteristics that have made him one of the most beloved figures in Akan folklore.

In one popular tale, Anansi is faced with a task that seems impossible: to gather all the world's wisdom and keep it for himself. Determined to be the wisest of all, Anansi sets out to collect wisdom from every corner of the land, hoarding it in a large pot he carries on his back. However, as he tries to climb a tree to hide his treasure, the pot becomes too heavy and slips, scattering wisdom across the land for all to share. This story highlights the Akan belief that wisdom is not meant to be hoarded or hidden but shared openly for the benefit of everyone. It serves as a reminder that those who try to keep knowledge for themselves will ultimately fail, as true wisdom comes from a willingness to learn and teach others. Through Anansi's failed attempt, the tale conveys that wisdom grows when it is shared, fostering a community where each person can learn from the insights of others.

In addition to teaching lessons about wisdom, Akan folktales often explore the concept of cunning as a tool for survival and success. In many stories, smaller or weaker characters use their cleverness to outwit larger, more powerful animals. In one such tale, a small but shrewd rabbit finds himself trapped in a pit with a ferocious leopard. While the leopard plans to attack, the rabbit quickly devises a plan, convincing the leopard that they should work together to escape. Once out of the pit, the rabbit immediately dashes to safety, leaving the bewildered leopard behind. This story emphasizes the Akan belief that intelligence and quick thinking can enable even the smallest and seemingly weakest to overcome daunting challenges. Cunning, when used wisely, is seen as a gift that levels the playing field, allowing individuals to navigate difficult situations where sheer strength alone would not be enough.

Folktales of wisdom and cunning are also used to teach important social values, such as cooperation, generosity, and respect for community. In another well-loved story, Anansi and Turtle are invited to a feast. Anansi, wanting to keep all the food for himself, tells Turtle he must wash his hands repeatedly before joining the table, causing him to miss the meal. Later, Turtle invites Anansi to a feast underwater, where Anansi, unable to hold his breath and reach the food, is left hungry. This story is a lesson in reciprocity and fairness, illustrating that selfishness can lead to one's own downfall. The Akan people use this tale to teach that cooperation and respect for others are essential for a balanced and harmonious life. Through Anansi's mischief and Turtle's response, the story demonstrates that actions often return to those who commit them, highlighting the idea of justice through natural consequences.

Wisdom and cunning in Akan folktales are not limited to strategies for outsmarting others; they also reveal the importance of understanding one's environment and adapting to change. Many stories emphasize that knowledge of the natural world, of other people, and of oneself is vital for survival and success. In a tale about a wise bird, the bird escapes from a hunter by offering three pieces of advice: never grieve over a lost opportunity, never believe the impossible, and never share valuable secrets with the wrong person. As soon as the hunter frees the bird to hear its advice, the bird reveals it holds a priceless gem but tells the hunter it is now too late to retrieve it. The hunter, frustrated, forgets the bird's first piece of advice and grieves over his loss. This tale teaches the value of applying wisdom in practical ways and of remaining grounded, even when faced with unexpected disappointments.

Folktales like these continue to inspire and instruct the Akan people, who see these stories as more than mere entertainment. They are a cultural inheritance, passed down through generations to impart life lessons and moral guidelines. In each tale, listeners are reminded of the strength that comes from resourcefulness and the importance of using one's mind to navigate life's challenges. By sharing these folktales, parents and elders instill values that will guide the younger generation, reinforcing the belief that cunning, tempered by wisdom and ethical conduct, is a powerful tool for personal and communal well-being.

Akan folktales often end with a moral or proverb that distills the story's lesson into a simple, memorable phrase, making it easier for listeners to recall the wisdom of the tale in daily life. These proverbs serve as concise expressions of cultural wisdom, capturing complex ideas about human behavior and social responsibility in a few words. They emphasize that cunning, though valuable, must be balanced by respect for others and a sense of justice. The Akan people understand that wisdom alone is not enough; it must be used in harmony with kindness, honesty, and respect for the community. The trickster figure, especially Anansi, exemplifies this idea by showing that cleverness without morality can lead to trouble, while intelligence grounded in compassion and fairness benefits all.

Through these folktales of wisdom and cunning, the Akan people celebrate the human spirit's resilience, adaptability, and capacity for insight. The stories reflect an understanding of life's complexities and the challenges of coexisting in a world filled with competing desires, goals, and personalities. They encourage listeners to think critically, act wisely, and approach situations with an open and adaptable mind. In every tale, there is an invitation to reflect, to learn, and to grow, as each character—whether animal or human—teaches a lesson about the possibilities of a mind that is both sharp and considerate. For the Akan, these folktales are a timeless reminder of the power of wisdom and the enduring importance of living with both intelligence and integrity.

Chapter 10: Anansi's Legacy in Akan Culture and Beyond

Anansi the Spider holds a lasting legacy in Akan culture and beyond, symbolizing not only the power of wit and cunning but also the enduring strength of storytelling as a means of passing down values, traditions, and cultural knowledge. As a trickster figure, Anansi is celebrated for his cleverness, his ability to use intelligence over brute strength, and his knack for finding unconventional solutions to problems. These qualities make him one of the most beloved characters in Akan folklore, where his stories are told in homes, community gatherings, and even ceremonial settings. His tales, known as *Anansesem*, serve as both entertainment and education, teaching children and adults alike about moral values, the consequences of selfish actions, and the importance of community and cooperation. Through his stories, Anansi becomes not only a character but a cultural hero whose exploits capture the complexities of human nature, offering lessons that remain relevant across generations.

Anansi's influence in Akan culture goes beyond mere storytelling; he is seen as a symbol of resilience and adaptability, qualities that resonate deeply with the Akan people. Living in a world where survival often depends on quick thinking and resourcefulness, the Akan have long valued these traits, finding in Anansi a character who embodies the ability to thrive even when faced with significant challenges. Many of Anansi's tales involve him encountering creatures stronger or more powerful than himself, yet he consistently uses his wit to gain the upper hand, proving that intelligence and strategic thinking are as valuable as physical strength. This aspect of Anansi's character reinforces the Akan belief that resilience and cleverness are essential tools for overcoming adversity. Anansi's legacy thus reinforces the notion that wisdom and adaptability are virtues to be celebrated and cultivated, as they enable individuals and communities to persevere through difficult times.

The legacy of Anansi has also crossed borders, traveling with the Akan people and other African communities through the transatlantic slave trade to the Caribbean, the Americas, and beyond. In the Caribbean, Anansi's stories took root in the cultures of enslaved African people, who found in him a symbol of resistance and survival. His tales became an oral tradition that connected African descendants with their heritage, offering them a means of expressing resistance to oppression and celebrating their ingenuity. Anansi became known as "Nancy" or "Anancy" in the Caribbean, where his stories adapted to local cultures, evolving to reflect the unique experiences and challenges faced by African communities in the diaspora. In Jamaica, for instance, Anansi is celebrated in folklore as a symbol of the ability to endure hardship and to resist the power structures imposed by colonialism. His tales offer humor and hope, reminding listeners of the strength found in resilience and the enduring power of one's heritage.

Through these migrations and adaptations, Anansi's legacy has continued to expand, evolving into new forms while maintaining his core characteristics of cleverness, resilience, and trickery. In African American culture, Anansi's influence can be seen in the Brer Rabbit stories of the American South, tales that similarly emphasize the value of intelligence over strength and the use of wit to overcome social and personal challenges. Though Brer Rabbit differs in appearance from Anansi, the spirit of the stories remains the same, with the trickster figure embodying the resilience of African heritage and the ingenuity needed to survive difficult circumstances. Anansi's tales have therefore played a crucial role in preserving African cultural values, providing a means of cultural continuity and identity for African descendants in the diaspora.

In contemporary literature and popular culture, Anansi continues to appear as a character who bridges traditional folklore with modern narratives. Authors such as Neil Gaiman, in his novel *Anansi Boys*, have reimagined Anansi, weaving his legacy into new stories that reach global audiences. In these modern retellings, Anansi retains his wit, his playful cunning, and his complex relationship with morality, serving as a reminder of the importance of tradition and storytelling in navigating modern life. Anansi's ability to adapt to different settings and cultures reinforces his relevance, showing that his legacy is not confined to the Akan or Caribbean cultures but resonates universally, as his qualities speak to the fundamental human experiences of survival, cleverness, and the power of narrative.

Anansi's legacy is also preserved through cultural festivals, performances, and educational programs, where his stories are told to celebrate African heritage and educate new generations about the values embedded in his tales. During events such as Kwanzaa, which emphasizes African cultural traditions and principles, Anansi's stories are often shared to highlight the value of creativity, community, and self-determination. These stories not only entertain but also encourage reflection on important themes, reminding listeners of the interconnectedness of individuals within a community and the role of storytelling in preserving cultural identity. By continuing to tell Anansi's tales, communities celebrate their roots, drawing from the lessons he represents to inspire and empower future generations.

In Akan culture, Anansi remains a beloved figure, one whose tales are considered cultural treasures, filled with humor, wisdom, and insights into human nature. He is a symbol of the Akan people's respect for knowledge, creativity, and resilience, serving as a reminder that intelligence and adaptability are as valuable as any physical strength. His stories often conclude with proverbs, distilling the wisdom of the tale into a single phrase or lesson that can be remembered and applied in daily life. These proverbs, like "Wisdom is like a baobab tree; no one individual can embrace it," reflect the Akan view that knowledge is collective and must be shared to benefit all. Anansi's tales thus reinforce the idea that wisdom and community go hand in hand, and that personal success is most meaningful when it is achieved with respect for others.

Anansi's legacy continues to inspire across time, geography, and generations, reflecting the universal themes of resilience, creativity, and morality that define his character. His tales are an enduring testament to the power of storytelling as a means of connecting people, bridging cultural gaps, and preserving the values of a society. Whether in the villages of Ghana, the streets of Jamaica, or the urban landscapes of North America, Anansi's stories remain a source of pride, cultural identity, and moral guidance, embodying a legacy that celebrates the ingenuity of the human spirit and the timeless wisdom of tradition.

Conclusion

In exploring the mythologies of the Yoruba, Dogon, Zulu, and Akan peoples, *Legends of Africa* has journeyed through the rich, diverse spiritual landscapes that have shaped African cultural heritage for centuries. Each mythology reveals a unique worldview, yet all share a profound reverence for nature, the cosmos, community, and the enduring power of the unseen. These stories connect people to their past, teaching valuable lessons about life, resilience, and the moral fabric of society.

In *Book 1*, *Orishas and Origins* unveils the Yoruba's complex pantheon of Orishas—deities of vibrant personality and divine power. The Orishas represent every facet of existence, governing human emotions, natural forces, and cosmic order. These tales teach that life is interconnected, with every action rippling through the universe, calling on humans to live in harmony with nature, honor their ancestors, and seek balance.

Book 2, *Stars and Spirits*, ventures into the Dogon's celestial-focused mythology, with its intricate beliefs about the Sirius star system, ancestral spirits, and the Nommo beings. This mythology showcases the Dogon's unique cosmology, interweaving spiritual insight with a deep understanding of the heavens. It reflects the Dogon's respect for mystery, knowledge, and the wisdom of ancestors, emphasizing humanity's place in the cosmic order.

In *Book 3*, *Thunders of the Sky* delves into Zulu mythology, where mighty gods, ancestral spirits, and heroic legends illustrate the people's reverence for courage, loyalty, and respect for elders. The stories of sky gods and legendary warriors reflect the Zulu's awe for the powerful forces of nature and the moral lessons taught through ancestral guidance. Through these tales, the Zulu people honor values that bind the community and uphold a sense of identity and strength.

Finally, *Book 4*, *Anansi's Web*, celebrates the Akan mythology of wisdom and cunning, with Anansi the Spider embodying resilience, adaptability, and the timeless art of storytelling. Anansi's tales emphasize the power of intelligence and wit, along with the Akan commitment to sharing wisdom for the benefit of all. These stories transcend time, uniting past and present generations in a legacy of humor, wit, and moral understanding.

Together, these mythologies provide a window into the soul of African spirituality and the values that have shaped communities over generations. They remind us that myths are not merely stories but timeless reflections of human aspirations, struggles, and triumphs. The sacred tales within these traditions serve as cultural guides, preserving the wisdom of ancestors and inspiring future generations to find meaning, strength, and unity in their heritage. Through the voices of these mythologies, *Legends of Africa* honors Africa's vast cultural legacy, inviting readers to embrace the universal truths and enduring wisdom that resonate across continents and generations.